Political Theology

Political Theology

A Critical Introduction

Saul Newman

polity

First published in 2019 by Polity Press   *BT*

Polity Press   *83.59*
65 Bridge Street
Cambridge CB2 1UR, UK   *.N49*
                                          2019

Polity Press
101 Station Landing
Suite 300
Medford, MA 02155, USA

ISBN-13: 978-1-5095-2839-4
ISBN-13: 978-1-5095-2840-0(pb)

A catalogue record for this book is available from the British Library.

Library of Congress Cataloging-in-Publication Data
Names: Newman, Saul, 1972- author.
Title: Political theology : a critical introduction / Saul Newman.
Description: Cambridge, UK ; Meford, MA : Polity, 2018. | Includes
    bibliographical references and index.
Identifiers: LCCN 2018009181 (print) | LCCN 2018027932 (ebook) |
    ISBN 9781509528431 (Epub) | ISBN 9781509528394 (hardback) |
    ISBN 9781509528400 (pbk.)
Subjects: LCSH: Political theology.
Classification: LCC BT83.59 (ebook) | LCC BT83.59 .N49 2018 (print) |
    DDC 261.7–dc23
LC record available at https://lccn.loc.gov/2018009181

Typeset in 11 on 13 pt Sabon by Toppan Best-set Premedia Limited
Printed and bound in Great Britain by Clays Ltd, Popson Street, Bungay
Elcograf S.p.A.

For further information on Polity, visit our website: politybooks.com

Contents

Acknowledgements

I would like to thank colleagues in the Sydney Democracy Network and the School of Social and Political Sciences at the University of Sydney, for their generous support in arranging a Visiting Professorship for me there while working on this book.

Introduction

Recent political phenomena all seem to be pointing to the end of the global liberal order. The resurgence of authoritarian, nationalist and anti-immigrant populism in Europe, the United States and elsewhere represents a major challenge to liberal values of openness, toleration and human rights. Everywhere these ideas and principles seem to be under attack, often from within the very heart of liberal democratic societies. Indeed, it would seem that a major rift has opened between liberalism and democracy itself, as significant parts of the demos, animated by a desire for a return of 'sovereignty', turn their backs on globalisation and multiculturalism and demand closed borders and a strong state. The spectre of national sovereignty has returned in our midst.

Sovereignty may be a phantasm, but this does not make its effects any less real. Indeed, in the era of globalisation, the problem of sovereignty becomes more acute. In a time when it is no longer possible for governments to exercise any real control over national economies, where vast sums of money are moved around the world in a blink of an eye and where an out-of-control banking system caused the near collapse of the global economy, it is hardly any wonder that many cling on to the idea of national sovereignty as their only salvation. Nor is it any surprise, perhaps, that many, the so called 'left behind', often attribute their sense of dislocation in the contemporary world to mass migration and to the fragmentation of their cultural and national identity that they believe to result from this. The renewed desire for a strong state and a unified, homogeneous identity can be seen as symptomatic of an increasingly abstracted and virtualised form of existence, where centres of power and sources of authority and legitimacy are more obscure and amorphous. What emerges here is the question of *who* is the sovereign, *who* decides. Is it the nation state, which represents, however indirectly, the will of the people? Or is it anonymous transnational legal structures and global financial networks?

This of course was the eternal question posed by Carl Schmitt, the conservative German jurist and political thinker who, is his 1922 book *Politische Theologie* (*Political Theology*), arrived at the famous – or infamous – formulation: '*Sovereign is he who decides on the exception*' (Schmitt, 2005: 5; emphasis added). For Schmitt, the authority to make decisions outside the law – in the liminal space of the exceptional situation that required the suspension of the normal constitutional order – was the ultimate and legitimate expression of sovereignty. If the sovereign cannot decide over and above what liberals affirm as the rule of law, then sovereignty is meaningless.

Moreover, for Schmitt, sovereignty is imbued with religious significance; it is a sacred concept, made all the more sacred in the time of secularism. Indeed, as a political theologian for whom modern concepts of the state are secularised theological concepts, Schmitt saw the sovereign as analogous with God as the supreme lawgiver, and the state of exception as akin to the miracle in theology. The sovereign is the redeemer and saviour of the people in a time of nihilism and political neutralisation, which is why at the same time it demands absolute obedience and sacrifice.

It is not my intention to side with Schmitt here – far from it. Despite a take-up in recent times by some thinkers on the left, who see Schmitt's theories as delimiting a space of differentiation and freedom in an international order dominated by liberal globalisation, or even as providing resources for a renewal and radicalisation of democratic politics (e.g., Mouffe, 2009), I see nothing positive or redemptive about any kind of return, were it even possible, to the bulwark of national sovereignty. However, where Schmitt is right is in pointing to the structural recurrence of the problematic of sovereignty, which is revealed every time a social order undergoes a crisis of legitimation – as the liberal order is currently experiencing. In this sense, the question of sovereignty – the desire for it, the identification with it – is in many ways central to politics and political thought. This does not mean that sovereignty is inescapable and that there are not alternative ways of organising social and political life – something I intend to explore in this book. However, we must first come to terms with the structural space or gap in our political language and experience that sovereignty both invokes and stands in for. Sovereignty points to a moment of transcendence beyond an otherwise immanent social order. Sovereignty represents an imaginary point of identity that fixes meaning and delineates borders and boundaries. It differentiates inside from outside, friend from enemy. It gives coherence and unity to society, providing a stabilising element in an unstable world. In the moment of crisis, the question of sovereignty becomes ever present as we try to re-create a sense of ontological certainty through the idea of transcendent authority. Yet, as I will aim to show, sovereignty is a dead end, a kind of trap that we must nevertheless navigate if we are to have any hope of overcoming the problem of political theology.

Yet what of sovereignty's supposedly restraining function in delaying the coming of the Antichrist – Schmitt's characterisation of the global disorder that would reign in the age of liberal economics, technological mobilisation and depoliticisation, in which the breakdown of the friend–enemy opposition defined by the nation state had the potential to result in violence on an unparalleled scale? Today it is difficult to

tell whether sovereignty serves as the *katechon* ('restrainer')
or *conductor* of the coming disorder. The apocalyptic and
nihilistic condition that Schmitt warned us of seems to be
coming about precisely through the breakup of the liberal
global order and uncanny return of the dream of sovereignty.
We need to understand this contemporary condition of nihilism and potential violence that lurks behind the edifice of the
sovereign state. It is the narrow, paranoid dream of identity
– national, cultural, religious – asserted against any univer-
salism. It is the obscure and nihilistic vision of the jihadist
who seeks to hasten the world's destruction, along with his
own. It is the politics of the nationalist, racist and identitar-
ian right that wants simply to turn its back on the world and
emphasise divisions between religions and cultures. It is the
populist Feast of Fools with its elected pope in the White
House, the pseudo-revolution against the liberal 'establishment'. It is the carnival that takes place at the end of times,
in a world faced with imminent ecological collapse. It is a
violent millenarianism without any promise of a Messiah.
Obscurantist and reactionary worldviews now take the place
of Enlightenment values of human rights, scientific truth,
toleration and secularism. The liberal consensus is in a state
of decomposition, and emerging in its place is an intensification of political enmity. There is a kind of *repoliticisation*
of our world going on, an intensification of what Schmitt
calls the 'friend–enemy' opposition, after decades of stifling,
technocratic neoliberalism. But this is not a politicisation
that holds out much hope of redemption, deteriorating into
a kind of 'identity politics' that animates the right and only
cripples the left.

   This book takes as its starting point our contemporary
post-liberal condition and what I have described as the phantasmatic 'return' of sovereignty. It will explore the crisis of
liberal politics and political theory through the problem of
political theology. Political theology, an enigmatic term, generally refers to the interpenetration of religion and politics.
More precisely, it refers to the way in which political concepts,
discourses and institutions – particularly sovereignty – are

influenced, shaped and underpinned by religious categories of thought. In some ways this is nothing new. Religion and politics have always been intertwined. The entire history of the Christian West, in its shifting relationship between religious and political power, between church and state, might be said to revolve around the politico-theological problem. The origins of the term 'political theology' derive from pre-Christian antiquity. The Roman scholar Marcus Terentius Varro (117–27 BC), knowledge of whose *Divine Antiquities* comes to us mainly from Augustine's *De civitate Dei*, drew a distinction between what he called civil theology and mythical and natural, theology, that is, between civic or political religion – the cult images that constituted the founding myths and religions of Rome and therefore had a *political* function – and mythical and natural religions (see Book 6 of *CD* in Augustine, 2014; also van Nuffelen, 2010). The term appears again, much later and in a very different context, in Spinoza's *Tractatus theologico-politicus*, written amid the religious conflicts of the seventeenth century (Spinoza, 2007). Here we find an attempt to separate philosophy – the space of reason and free enquiry – from religious faith and scriptural determination, which Spinoza believed led to superstition and blind obedience. This separation should be preserved by the state and protected from intrusion by fanatical clergy. Yet, while Spinoza's thinking points towards a form of separation between religion and politics, church and state, he nevertheless acknowledged the political utility of religion in promoting allegiance to the state.

However, in the modern period, the term 'political theology' has come to be irrecoverably associated with Carl Schmitt, for whom the ambivalent and problematic relationship between religion and politics had become more acute in the time of secularism. The process of separating state from church and politics from religion, which began in the sixteenth century, had reached its high point when Schmitt was writing in the twentieth century. Yet, as he sought to show, the political categories that define the modern state are really theological concepts, which are translated into secular language but continue to bear the trace of their religious roots: '*All significant concepts of the modern theory of the state are secularized theological concepts*' (Schmitt, 2005: 36; emphasis added). Not only did sovereignty, as supreme law-making authority, develop from religion – from the idea of the sovereignty of God over natural law and its articulation into the doctrine of the divine right of kings – but the concept of sovereignty is fundamentally structured in this theological way. Or at least it must be so perceived – as the ultimate authority to decide, over and above the law – if it is to have any coherence in the modern world. However – and this is the real problem for Schmitt – this notion of sovereignty was under threat, not only from legal positivists and liberal constitutionalists, who wanted to demonstrate the pre-eminence of law over sovereignty and rule out the state of exception, but also from modern sociological and positivist explanations, which saw social relations in terms of pure immanence without any point of metaphysical transcendence or the sacred. Yet the greatest threat to the theological pre-eminence and absolutism of sovereignty came, according to Schmitt, from atheistic revolutionary anarchism, which declared total war on God and the state.

I will explore these debates in greater detail in chapter 1. But what becomes clear is the way in which secularism – the process by which religion and politics, church and state become formally separated – actually accentuates the politico-theological paradigm that Schmitt is exploring. Schmitt appears to be saying two things that seem, at first glance, to be in tension with each other: first, that secularism never really was entirely secular, in the sense that its political categories still bear the trace of their religious origins and are still steeped in theology; and, secondly, that in secular modernity – with its forces of atheism, positivism, liberal economics, technics, and revolutionary politics – transcendence becomes increasingly impossible and that there is indeed a mortal threat to the sacred, absolute dimension of the sovereign state, which must therefore be bolstered and strengthened in response. One finds in Schmitt an affirmation of the theological intensity of sovereignty – the reactionary Catholic's desire to restore the authority and lustre of the state as *corpus mysticum* or sacred body – coupled with a kind of melancholic nostalgia for its lost pre-eminence in secular modernity.

Let us try to make sense of the contemporary implications of the politico-theological problem that Schmitt introduces. How does this help us to understand our current predicament? In what sense is our political reality still haunted by religion? To what extent does the apparition of God linger on behind the visage of sovereignty, even in these supposedly secular times? Or is it the case that the renewed desire for sovereignty is indicative of a deeper crisis in secular modernity and points to the 'return' of religion? To what extent does the force of religion – which, one might argue, never really went away – gather like a storm behind the edifice of the sovereign state and emerge in all its violent intensity at moments when the political order undergoes a crisis of legitimacy? In the time defined by the death of God, does God continue to live on in spectral form in the idea of sovereignty and political authority? In any case, Nietzsche believed that people would be unable to come to terms with the death of God and would try to reinvent him in the form of moral ideals derived from Christianity. This drive to restore divine authority in secular garb is something I will explore throughout the book.

Of course, the persistence of the problem of political theology raises important questions about secularism itself. Can we still maintain that we live, as Charles Taylor (2007) put it, in a secular age? Secularism, deriving from the Latin *saeculum* – referring to a certain length of time, a generation – is usually associated today with the institutional separation of church and state and the general evacuation of religion from the public into the private sphere; a process that started with the Protestant Reformation in the sixteenth century and early ideas of religious toleration and was intensified by the scientific revolutions of the seventeenth century and by the Enlightenment revolt of reason and political liberty against religious obscurantism and absolutism that characterised the eighteenth and nineteenth centuries. It is difficult not to acknowledge the fundamental changes that have taken place during this time, when compared with an earlier period in which religion was much more deeply ingrained in everyday life. Today public institutions, at least in modern western societies, no longer draw their legitimacy from the church – or, if they do, it is in only in a highly symbolic and not substantive way. Religious faith has become a matter of personal choice rather than obligation. Religion no longer serves as a source of authority for law and morality, and public displays of religiosity tend to be regarded as anomalies rather than the norm. Max Weber refers to the experience of 'disenchantment' in secular modernity – a general process of demystification and rationalisation of social life, whereby religion is progressively relegated to the sphere of private belief and public authority derives its legitimacy from other sources, such as the rule of law and bureaucratic efficiency. Taylor characterises secularism as a change in the background conditions of belief: it may be that some people, indeed many, hold strong religious beliefs, but this is simply a matter of personal choice and indeed one option among many – including non-belief, which is more likely to be the default position today. Moreover, for Taylor, a self-sufficient humanism has come to supplant the experience of spiritual and metaphysical transcendence. In other words, today it is possible to derive one's sense of fullness entirely *within* the human condition and to think of no higher goal than purely human flourishing – whereas in earlier, pre-secular society this sense of fullness could only come from something transcendent, beyond the limits of human experience (ibid., 19–20).

At the same time, however, secularism has become an increasingly contested notion, and debates in recent years in political theory and continental philosophy – particularly in the wake of 9/11 – have revolved around what has come to be known as the 'post-secular'. This has been partly in recognition of a world in which religion seems to have 'returned' to the public sphere, in often fundamentalist and violent forms, and now seriously threatens the secular political space. Can we really say that we live in a secular world when terrorist attacks, inspired by fundamentalist interpretations of religion, occur with ever greater frequency in the heart of liberal democratic societies, and when there are people who are prepared to sacrifice their own lives and those of others on the altar of their religious beliefs? To what extent can we say we have successfully and irreversibly separated church and state when, for instance, evangelical Christianity and other religiously conservative movements have such inordinate influence on electoral politics and government policy in the United States and other parts of the world? In what sense is the public space really free from religion, when there are major debates, becoming more vitriolic by the day, about the incompatibility of different religions and cultures and the impossibility of peaceful coexistence? The 'post-secular' condition has therefore become the context for rethinking the relationship between religion, culture and politics and for a critical reflection on the meaning of secularism.[1]

For Jürgen Habermas (2008), the 'post-secular' refers to a different sensibility, which he attributes to several factors: a heightened awareness of the religious dimension of global conflicts, something that brings into sharp relief the limits of the secular; the increased influence of religion in the public sphere; and immigration from countries with more traditionally bound cultures, presenting challenges of integration and highlighting tensions between religious pluralism and the secular public space. The central problem for post-secular societies is how to mediate the conflict between religious differences and the democratic public space, which tolerates differences but does so only on the basis of a shared allegiance to a secular notion of citizenship that requires distancing oneself from one's cultural and religious particularity. There seems to be an almost irresolvable tension between the identity of the religious minority demanding recognition in a secular society and the defenders of a rigid secularism, a position that itself devolves into another kind of identity politics, a 'fundamentalism of the Enlightenment', whose formal discourse of 'toleration' takes an increasingly intolerant tone and whose proclaimed secularism increasingly falls back on claims about the superiority of 'western culture', with its Christian roots, over Islam. We see this in endless debates in the West over multiculturalism, sharia law, the veil, religious offence, and freedom of speech.

Therefore the danger to secularism comes not only from the fact that religious differences are not able to accommodate themselves to secular principles, but also from a narrow and intolerant interpretation of secularism itself. For Habermas (2008), if the secular space is to survive, it must adapt itself to the realities of religious pluralism; indeed, if equal recognition is to mean anything, then secularists must no longer expect that their religious fellow citizens leave their religious affiliations at the door when they enter the public political space. Secularists must be able to recognise the political validity of deeply held religious convictions. A similar attempt to accommodate religious pluralism within secular societies was proposed earlier by John Rawls (2005), who made a distinction between public reason and secular reason. While secular reason seeks to exclude religion from politics altogether, public reason accepts the place of deeply held religious convictions in public political debates, provided these debates took place in terms that all reasonable and rational people, believers and non-believers alike, might understand and agree to; that there is, in other words, a rational common ground that might allow a resolution of such conflicts. It is thus possible to establish, according to Rawls, an overlapping consensus of 'reasonable' comprehensive doctrines – a more substantive agreement than a simple *modus vivendi* between irreconcilable positions. This consensus served therefore as a more stable basis for contemporary liberal societies, while at the same time respecting religious differences. Both Rawls and Habermas seek to come to terms with religious pluralism through a certain modification of the idea of the secular public space, accommodating religious differences within a constitutional regime that nevertheless derives its legitimacy from secular principles of equal recognition of citizens as reasonable and rational.

Other thinkers, however, have raised more serious questions about the idea of western secular liberal reason. Talal Asad's genealogy of secular reason calls into question the concept of the secular West as an integrated totality, seeing it instead as a heterogeneous and conflicted notion, riven by tensions and inconsistencies, whose self-identity as 'rational' and 'tolerant' is formed through a problematic distinction from various forms of 'irrational' and 'intolerant' fundamentalism. Moreover, western secular modernity, according to Asad, is based on a questionable opposition between the religious and the secular, the sacred and the profane, elements that in fact interpenetrate each other. Secularism promises a story of redemption – one that is different from Christian theology but nevertheless contains a sacrificial logic prepared to inflict suffering in the name of humanisation (Asad, 2003: 62). For instance, insofar as human rights can only be enforced through the nation state, states have the power to coerce their own citizens – and indeed others outside their boundaries – in the name of human rights. Secular, universal human rights are thus caught up in the very paradox of sovereignty; entirely reliant as they are on the sovereign nation state for their enforcement, they place themselves at the mercy of the entity they were designed to protect individuals from in the first place.

Jacques Derrida is another thinker for whom the concept of the secular, insofar as it defines itself in opposition to the religious, should be questioned. Indeed, the very notion of religion as a singular, coherent, meaningful category is impossible to sustain, as is the distinction between reason and religion, knowledge and faith. These forces share a common origin and have an entangled history, which today plays itself out in the form of tensions inherent in western globalisation – or what Derrida calls 'globalatinisation'. We see, for instance, the way in which globalisation is perceived by some as a threat to their religious identity, while at the same time religious doctrines are spread and promulgated through communication technologies and pathways made available by globalisation. For Derrida, we cannot hope to understand the phenomenon of the 'return of the religious' today if we insist on the naïve opposition between reason, science and modernity on the one hand and religion on the other (Derrida, 1998: 28). Indeed, we cannot possibly come to terms with what Derrida calls the new 'wars of religion' – a phenomenon that today, nearly two decades since his writing, seem only to be intensifying – without understanding the mutual interpenetration of western secular reason, which increasingly takes the form of a techno-scientific rationality, with religion. Secular reason cannot be strictly separated or isolated from a religious dimension latent in the theological Judeo-Christian foundations of the West. The point Derrida is making is that the secular domain cannot be in any sense purified of the religious; even the political domain – and here we return to Schmitt – relies upon the heteronymous dimension of the theological in order to achieve any 'autonomy' (ibid., 25–6).

We can see, then, that secularism is a highly contested concept and that its status today is uncertain. How can the paradigm of political theology help us to make sense of this matter? Let us turn briefly to one of the central debates over the secularisation hypothesis – the twentieth-century debate between Karl Löwith and Hans Blumenberg over the meaning and significance of modernity. For Löwith, modernity and the idea of progress are nothing but a form of secularised Christian eschatology. Our modern belief in universal progress – particularly the idea that history has some kind of ultimate meaning or purpose – is still structured by a prophetic and messianic promise of redemption and salvation familiar to us from the Jewish and Christian traditions. Modern historicism has Judeo-Christian origins, and we moderns, in our search for a *telos* or final goal of history, are simply heirs to this Christian eschatology. We are governed by an 'eschatological compass' that 'gives orientation in time by pointing to the Kingdom of God as the ultimate end or purpose' (Löwith, 1949: 18). This theological parallel is quite evident, for instance, in the revolutionary eschatology of Marx: the history of exploitation is the history of injustice and evil, an evil that will be finally overcome in the messianic promise of communism, a new kind of 'kingdom of God' on earth. For Löwith, then, the modern world, even in its radical atheism and secularism, still remains in the shadow of Christianity and is still structured by its eschatological horizon. Secularism is the fulfilment of Christianity; and yet, in this fulfilment, it also dissolves Christianity by applying it to secular matters (ibid., 202).[2]

Hans Blumenberg (1985), on the other hand, rejects Löwith's sceptical interpretation of modernity and progress. The thesis that everything about the modern age, including its political concepts and institutions, is simply a secularisation of Christian theology and eschatology was overstated and simplistic, based as it was on a blind spot that failed to recognise the specificity and originality of modernity. Rather than searching for the theological spirit behind the appearance of 'wordliness', we should affirm the legitimacy of the modern age as an autonomous experience and as a novel response to the breakdown of the medieval Christian world. For instance, the idea of progress, which Löwith sees merely as a secularised form of the Christian motif of salvation, was actually, according to Blumenberg, a distinct and uniquely modern alternative to a Christian eschatology that had come to be not so much about hope as about terror and dread of the next world (ibid., 31). The modern world, a world now reliant only on itself and its own conceptual resources – abandoned, as Blumenberg puts it, to its own self-assertion – reoccupied the void left empty by an eschatological narrative that had long since ceased to function and could no longer promise any Messiah. Therefore '[t]his true "creation of the world" [*Weltwerdung*] is not a secularization ("becoming worldly") in the sense of the transformation of something preexisting but rather, as it were, the primary crystallization of a hitherto unknown reality' (ibid., 47). *This* world, in all its newness and innovation, had come to take the place of

the *other* world, the old world of Christian theology abandoned by any hope of salvation. Modern reason in the form
of philosophy now had to find answers to the questions and
mysteries left unresolved by theology.

It is not surprising, then, that Blumenberg was critical of
Schmitt's deployment of the secularisation thesis to justify
his claim for absolute sovereignty: the political theologian
needed the concept of a secularised theology in order to
claim that the sovereign has, or *should have*, God-like
authority today. However, as Blumenberg points out, this
absolutist idea of political authority is out of kilter with the
modern age, an age where the state of emergency – what
Schmitt calls the exception – is no longer the 'normal' condition of politics and where the notion of 'the political' loses
its primacy (ibid., 91). Schmitt must therefore call on a theological absolutism if he is to bring back to life the idea of
political absolutism; but he does so in a spurious way, relying
on a series of structural analogies to justify his claims. 'Political theology' was therefore only a metaphorical theology.
According to Blumenberg, Schmitt was not so much a 'political theologian' as a political theorist making a rhetorical
case and calling on theological images to affirm a strong
sovereign (ibid., 101).

I will return to some of these points, particularly about the
distinction between political theology and political theory,
in chapter 1. However, we can see how Blumenberg's critique of the secularisation thesis – his critique of the idea
that secular modernity is simply a transposition and continuation of Christianity – would seem to cast doubt on the
very concept of political theology. Or does it? The fact that
modernity, for Blumenberg, takes over in the wake of the disintegration of Christian theology – he refers to a 'reoccupa-
tion' (ibid., 89) – suggests that modernity, or what I refer to
as secular modernity, is at the very least premised on Christian theology, even if it only fills the place left vacant by it. To
the extent that modern philosophy and political theory seek
to answer the questions left unresolved by Christian theology, suggests that they are still in some ways shaped by it,

even as they may seek to distance themselves from it. Insofar as modernity is an aggressive self-assertion of a radically new attitude that emerges as a critical response to Christian theology, we can say that it is formed and constituted in opposition to it. My point is that, at the end of the day, there is not such a huge difference between Löwith's and Blumenberg's positions in terms of their implications for political theology: both point to a place of transcendence, which is invoked, in Löwith's case, as the continuation of Christian eschatology in secular modernity and, in Blumenberg's case, in the form of its absence, a void that the conceptual and political resources of modernity try to fill. To refer to this place of transcendence is not to invoke the name of God or to lament his absence from secular modernity. Rather I am referring to a kind of structural gap or lack in the symbolic order, which characterises any society but becomes particularly acute and visible in the wake of secular modernity and the breakup of the old medieval theological order. The recurrent desire for ever stronger forms of sovereignty can be seen in some ways as a desire for fullness and wholeness in political life – for the sacred in the secular experience.

Rather than taking a particular position, then, on the secularisation debate, my point will be that the problem of political theology should be considered as a symptom of our secular modernity; indeed, that it only really arises with, and as a consequence of, the formal separation of religion and politics that characterises modernity and that dissolved the symbolic consistency of the medieval order. The place of political authority is inclined to take on a theological dimension precisely at the same time as its legitimacy is called into question, as it was with the decomposition of the old cosmic political order and the discrediting of the doctrine of divine right – and, indeed, as it is today, in the age of liberal globalisation. So why is it that political authority – the state order – becomes theologised precisely at the moment when religion becomes depoliticised, when it is banished from the public sphere into the private sphere? This was something that Marx commented on in his discussion of liberal secularism.

In his critique of the secularising arguments of his contemporary Bruno Bauer, Marx reflected on the paradox whereby the liberal state, once it reached full political maturity – in other words, once it emancipated itself from religion and became fully secular – takes on a theological position in relation to the rest of society: 'The political state, in relation to civil society, is just as spiritual as is heaven in relation to earth. It stands in the same opposition to civil society, and overcomes it in the same manner as religion overcomes the narrowness of the profane world' (Marx, 1978: 34). The state now occupies the place of theological transcendence once occupied by the church and formal religion. The depoliticisation of theology leads only to the *theologisation* of politics. The state's abandonment of religion – the abolition of religion from the public political domain – leads only to the religion of the state. Therefore the public–private divide, central to liberal secularism, does not dissolve religion: it only entrenches religion more firmly in private life, while at the same time creating a new secular religion: the religion of the state. Of course, for Marx, the real problem was neither that of religion nor that of the state, but rather the way in which liberal secularism and the public–private divide integrate the forces of the market within civil society such that we are reduced, in the private sphere, to the status of a commodity and thus become 'the plaything of alien powers' (ibid.). This is a point I shall return to when I explore the question of *economic* theology in a later chapter. However, it is important to note that, for Marx, religious illusion serves as a kind of analytical matrix for thinking about ideology and politics; and from this we can gain an understanding of the theological dimension of power in secular modernity.

Moreover, that political power derives its legitimacy from democracy in modernity does not make it any less theological. Indeed, the symbolic authority of the 'will of the people' does not desacralise power at all but, on the contrary, makes it all the more transcendent. Tocqueville famously observed about American democracy in the nineteenth century: 'The people rule the American political world as God rules the universe. They are the cause and the end of all things; everything arises from them and everything is absorbed by them' (de Tocqueville 2010: 97). This was a new kind of despotism. Behind every modern conception of sovereignty, starting with Hobbes, there is the figure of the people, who are represented, no matter how indirectly, by the state. Even Schmitt sees the sovereign state as being the entity that constitutes and galvanises the people, uniting them against their common enemy. The democratic *pouvoir constituant* – the sovereign power over laws that flows from the people – is by no means antithetical to transcendence and therefore cannot be an answer, at least not on its own, to the problem of political theology. Recent expressions of demotic power whose 'will' must be obeyed absolutely, lest one be declared an 'enemy of the people',[3] are an example of this theological spectre that haunts modern politics and brings renewed focus on its foundations and legitimacy.

So we can say that the problem of political theology is a way of thinking about the foundations and legitimacy of power in modern societies. And it is something that becomes particularly acute when the symbolic order of society – the structures of authority that ground the social order and maintain its coherence – break down and experience a crisis of legitimacy. This is what accounts for what Claude Lefort calls the permanence of the theologico-political in secular society:

> Can we not admit that, despite all the changes that have occurred, the religious survives in the guise of new beliefs and new representations, and that it can therefore return to the surface, in either traditional or novel forms, when conflicts become so acute as to produce cracks in the edifice of the state? (Lefort, 2006: 150)

For Lefort, modern democratic society, which was formed in the eighteenth century, removed the ontological certainties of previous orders and based itself instead on heterogeneity and division; it is structured by a symbolically empty place of power, left vacant by the absent body of the prince. As a result of the democratic revolutions of the eighteenth and nineteenth centuries, which according to Lefort split the orders of power, law and knowledge, society could no longer be represented as a single, unified body. However, this empty space of contingency created at the same time a desire for absolute foundations, for a point of transcendence – once provided by religion – that could unify a fragmented social order and master this experience of uncertainty. The persistence of religion is therefore a symptom of the uncertainty and contingency at the foundations of democratic society. This is also why, at various times, ideas of nation, community and people become substitutes for religion, attempting to fill the empty space of power and unify society. For Schmitt, sovereignty fulfils precisely this function. Such ideas, which as Lefort believes speak to a real, yet unavoidable, structural deficit in society, appear at moments when a perceived loss of legitimacy is seen to threaten the social order. The survival of religion itself in modern society – which now works on an imaginary rather than symbolic register – evokes the illusion that firm identity and absolute unity can be restored. The constant danger, for Lefort, is that these representations of identity become so invested with desire that they open the way to a totalitarian drive to forcibly reunite the social order (ibid., 167).

Whether our society today is at risk of a new kind of totalitarian politics is perhaps too early to tell, although some signs are there. Schmitt was certainly not immune to this temptation. However, the important point being made by Lefort here is that the division between religion and politics, worked out over many centuries – the long process by which the *corpus mysticum* of the church was incarnated in the political body of the king and then passed to the new political body of the people – left a kind of theological trace or remnant that haunts the modern political space. This is not to say that modern secular democracy is simply a transferral of religion from one register to another. Rather, religion persists in the form of its own absence, circumscribing an empty space in the social order and invoking the continual desire for a point of transcendence that is embodied in new forms of power.

My overall argument in this book is that political theology is not so much a problem of religion in modern societies as a problem of *power* – not only, as we shall go on to see, the power embodied in the concept of sovereignty, but also the new forms of governmental, economic and technological power that emerge with the modern state. Religion, in its *absent presence* in modern societies, creates a space of transcendence in which new forms of power emerge and proliferate. The space left by the disappearance of religion from the public political space is the structural void that modern forms of power try to fill, essentially reoccupying its position of transcendence. The fact that, in recent times, we have been witness to the 'return' of religion in the public domain is symptomatic of a certain breakdown or inconsistency in the symbolic order of society – an inconsistency that power tries to resolve or cover up by absorbing into itself the imaginary transcendence once supplied by religion. This is not to say that power does not, at times, call upon religious ideology in a more overt way; in fact it often does. However, political theology refers to the much more subtle way in which power fills the space left vacant by religion and, in so doing, draws into itself, into its structures and legitimising discourses and orders of truth, religion's transcendent dimension. We should understand power as a form of transcendence, or indeed as the form that transcendence now takes in modern societies. *Rather than religion becoming power, power becomes religion.* If this is the case, we will not resolve the deadlock of political theology – the seemingly inextricable bind between theology and politics – until we find ways of displacing, escaping and transcending the forms of power that govern us in modern societies and, in one way or another, call for our continual obedience and sacrifice.

The other question I seek to address in this book is the relationship between political theology and political philosophy, or, as Leo Strauss (1967) put it, between the two poles of Jerusalem and Athens that have defined the intellectual tradition of the West. In his own reflections on the politico-theological problem, on which more will be said in the next chapter, Strauss drew upon a central distinction between a form of thought that took its truth from revelation and saw wisdom in faith and obedience to its one message, and a way of thinking based on free, rational questioning, guided by the eternal goal of justice. Prophecy and reason, faith and enquiry, obedience and freedom, authority and justice have been the two incompatible modes of thought – theological and philosophical – that have formed our contemplation of politics. While we must be able to differentiate between these modes of thinking, I would argue that any genuine philosophical reflection on the state of politics today cannot escape the encounter with political theology. If we are to reflect critically on the limitations of our conceptual language for dealing with the problems we face – if we are to enquire into the suitability today of concepts such as freedom, democracy, rights, community and sovereignty – we need to understand the ways in which our political language has been penetrated and suffused by theological spectres. For Strauss (2007), while the role of philosophy is not to change the world but to interpret it, philosophy is nevertheless needed when political action starts to be led astray by erroneous ideas. While it is not as simple as correcting the theological illusions that currently lead politics astray – rather it is a matter of working through and exploring the reasons for their entanglement – it seems to me that the age-old vocation of political philosophy has never been more urgent.

1

The Politico-Theological Problem

In the hope – a vain one perhaps – of stealing a march on political theology and routing it from the outset, I propose to begin the discussion of this topic from an unexpected place. While it is customary to start with Schmitt and his now famous 1922 work *Politische Theologie* (Schmitt, 2005), I want to take as my point of departure an earlier figure, whose political commitments could not be more different from the German jurist's. It is not often recognised that the term 'political theology', commonly attributed to Schmitt, actually comes, at least in its modern variation, from the nineteenth-century Russian anarchist Mikhail Bakunin. In a polemical essay from 1871 titled 'La théologie politique de Mazzini et l'Internationale', Bakunin reproaches the great Italian politician and republican Guiseppe Mazzini for illegitimately mixing religion and politics. Mazzini's revolutionary role in the formation of the Italian state was marred, for Bakunin, by his Christianity and religious idealism – a theological abstraction that led him to turn against the cause of human emancipation and progress. Mazzini was the 'last high priest of religious, metaphysical, and political idealism which is disappearing' (Bakunin, 1871).

The idealist, whether of the religious, philosophical or political kind – it is all the same to Bakunin – is one who abstracts moral principles from the materiality of life, suspending them above the living forces of society, as if from heaven over earth, and turning them against humanity. That is why, according to Bakunin, religion has usually been on the side of the state, why the theologian is also a political absolutist, and why sovereignty has cloaked itself in religious ideology. Just as God transcends the world and nature, the state transcends and stands above society; the same principle of absolute sovereignty is at work in both. Moreover, the reason why religious idealists and political absolutists reach the same conclusions is that both proceed from the doctrine of original sin, which leads them to the same 'melancholy destiny': man is not to be trusted, and therefore needs the moral authority of religion and the political authority which can only come from a strong state. Schmitt, as we shall see, reasons in exactly this way. This metaphysical abstraction from the real world is intolerable to Bakunin, and it was his outrage at this that led him to declare himself on the side of Satan in his rebellion against God's authority. Satan was the first real humanist and anarchist. Modern revolutions – exemplified by the Paris Commune of 1871 – were thus 'the audacious realization of the Satanic myth, a revolt against God; and today as always the two opposing parties are ranged, the one under the standard of Satan or of liberty, the other under the divine banner of authority' (Bakunin, 1971). For Bakunin, we are confronted with a great conflict between the forces of idealism and political reaction (the church, state and capital, shrouded in phantasms, with their assorted array of ideologues, metaphysicians and political theologians such as Mazzini – but there are worse) and the progressive forces of materialism, atheism, internationalism and revolutionary socialism, which in the end will prevail.

Bakunin's implacable critique of political theology[1] is of major concern to Schmitt. Indeed, Bakunin is revealed in *Political Theology* and elsewhere as one of Schmitt's chief antagonists, one who best represents modernity's assault on the sanctity of the state. In fact I would go as far as to suggest that Schmitt's whole politico-theological apparatus and his theory of the sovereign state of exception are mobilised precisely against the threat posed by the kind of atheistic and materialist revolutionary politics that Bakunin represents. If there is a relationship of enmity at work in Schmitt's political theology, Bakunin and the anti-politico-theological gesture of revolutionary anarchism emerge as the real enemy.

I will return to this question later. However, it will be the aim of this chapter to explore Schmitt's particular and highly influential interpretation of political theology and to understand the kinds of questions and problems he was responding to. Schmitt's at times enigmatic account of political theology will be clarified by exploring a number of debates – not only with anarchism (with which there could be no 'debate' as such, only outright war, something akin to a religious war), but also with key interlocutors such as Leo Strauss, the theologian Erik Peterson, and the Jewish philosopher Jacob Taubes. Here I will illustrate my central thesis that the problem of political theology is really the problem of power itself.

Political Theology

Schmitt wrote his *Political Theology* at a time of political crisis – in some ways like our own time. His work can be seen as a response to the lack of legitimacy of the Weimar Republic, a political order weakened and destabilised not only by economic dislocation and hyperinflation, but also by the forces of political radicalism. However, for the conservative Weimar jurist, this instability was indicative of the deeper crisis of liberal modernity, in which atheism, capitalism and technology worked to neutralise the dimension of the political and to deny modern societies a place of transcendence that was once provided by religion.[2] Indeed, the constitutional liberal state was itself an embodiment of this nihilism and loss of political meaning – it had become, or was in danger of becoming, a mere administrative machine

without genuine political substance and without a transcendent or sacred dimension that would act as a point of legitimacy for public order. What was missing in the Weimar state
was the 'spirit' of sovereignty, which was essential to any
genuine political order. Schmitt is concerned above all with
the need for a stable order in society, something that could
only be achieved through a coherent political form or 'idea'.
It was this that led Schmitt to affirm an authoritarian and
decisionist account of sovereignty and that explains, at least
in part, his attraction to Nazism some years later. Schmitt's
decision to republish *Political Theology* in 1934 may be seen
in the context of his political support for the Nazi regime,
which had recently come to power, and his seeing the Nazi
(counter)revolution as the redemption and salvation of the
German state.[3]

Schmitt's return to the theme of political theology many
years later shows that the connection between religion and
politics was a question that preoccupied him throughout his
life. As a political theologian, his concern is to understand
the conditions of secularism and the threat it poses to politics, as well as to find new sources of political authority and
legitimacy. In other words, modern secularism makes the
politico-theological problem – the loss of transcendence in
society – particularly acute. Influenced by Max Weber,
Schmitt accepted the secularisation hypothesis although he
rejected its liberal conclusions. In other words, he accepted
the idea that modernity is founded on a progressive secularisation of religious concepts and categories resulting in an
experience of 'disenchantment' – a loss of a sacred, transcendent dimension in society. Schmitt's (2005: 36) own
version of the secularisation thesis is summarised in the
following oft-quoted passage in *Political Theology*:

> All significant concepts of the modern theory of the state are
> secularized theological concepts not only because of their
> historical development – in which they were transferred from
> theology to the theory of the state, whereby, for example,
> the omnipotent God became the omnipotent lawgiver – but

also because of their systematic structure, the recognition of which is necessary for a sociological consideration of these concepts. The exception in jurisprudence is analogous to the miracle in theology.

Schmitt proposes a 'sociology' of political and juristic concepts based on a series of analogies with theological categories. Just as Bakunin perceived in his anti-political theology, there was, for Schmitt, a clear structural parallel between the absolute authority of God and the absolute authority of the sovereign; similarly, the state of exception – in which the legal constitution is suspended by the sovereign's decision – is similar to God's miracle that suspends the laws of nature.

By highlighting these structural analogies, Schmitt is not so much reflecting on the persistence of religion in politics, but rather pointing to the place of transcendence left vacant by the collapse of the theological world in the sixteenth century and to the way in which secular political concepts of the state have subsequently struggled to fill this void. Once again, religion and theology are present in modernity precisely in the form of their absence – an absence that leaves an indelible trace on our political experience. As theological authority diminishes, there are a series of displacements and substitutions of its conceptual categories, which find their way into the historical understanding of sovereignty and create a place of transcendence that allows a political order to be instituted: 'To the conception of God in the seventeenth and eighteenth centuries belongs the idea of his transcendence vis-à-vis the world, just as to that period's philosophy of state belongs the notion of the transcendence of the sovereign vis-à-vis the state' (Schmitt, 2005: 49). Thus, in the seventeenth century – in the age of deism, in which natural law supplanted the miracle – it was still possible to think of God as the sovereign architect of the world; Leviathan was still a 'mortal god'. And even in the eighteenth century, the age of Enlightenment rationalism, one finds theological ideas creeping, for instance, into Rousseau's divine-like legislator.

There is a politicisation of theological concepts as a way of speaking about sovereignty.

However, this way of thinking becomes increasingly impossible in the nineteenth century, which Schmitt characterises as the age of immanence. Here, under the influence of liberal economics, atheistic materialism and new scientific modes of investigation, the world comes to coincide entirely with itself and there is no longer space for transcendence, in either a theological or a political sense. Thus, in the modern concept of democracy, in which the division between ruler and ruled is eclipsed, as well as in modern liberal concepts of the state, in which the sovereign coincides absolutely with the state and the state coincides absolutely with the law, the traditional idea of the sovereign as standing above society becomes untenable (Schmitt, 2005: 49–50). In this flattened-out world there can be no place for hierarchy or genuine authority. Schmitt suggests, and here I agree with him, that immanence and materialism are themselves a new kind of metaphysics; this is something I shall take up in subsequent chapters. However, for Schmitt, the political implications of the modern age of materialism – which is seen as the fulfilment of the process of secularisation – are serious indeed: the loss of transcendence means the loss of political legitimacy.

However, why does the breakdown of theological constructs lead to a loss of political legitimacy? Why cannot other sources of legitimacy be found in a constitutional order, for instance, as liberals in Schmitt's time and in ours would propose? For Schmitt, attempts in modernity to reoccupy the void left by theology are mostly unsuccessful because they lack what he called a coherent political 'idea' and therefore have no capacity for representation. In *Roman Catholicism and Political Form* (Schmitt, 1996b), written at the same time as *Political Theology*, Schmitt argues that the unifying political form or idea was once provided, in the sixteenth century, by the Catholic Church and papal *auctoritas*. The Catholic Church had the capacity for *representation* – it could offer a unified image of the social order as embodied or incarnated in the Person of Christ. The idea of the person is really central to representation, and therefore to political legitimacy: it is only a person that can assume a definite form, and thus represent other persons; it is only a person that could embody political authority. This was something Hobbes understood well, which is why he had to invent Leviathan, a gigantic and artificial person to represent and thus institute the political order. The reason why, according to Schmitt, modern political institutions lack this representative capacity is that materialism, in its undifferentiated immanence of economic production and consumption, cannot form a person. In other words, it cannot generate a definitive political form that could convey personal authority and *dignitas*. Modern bourgeois societies are saturated by private individualism and lack any concept of the public political form. They can only generate anonymous functionaries who operate as nodes in a gigantic administrative and mercantile machine: 'The merchant sits in his office; the savant, in his study or laboratory. If they are really modern, both serve a factory – both are anonymous. It is senseless to claim they represent something' (Schmitt, 1996b: 20).

Exception and Norm

Here we can see the Weberian disappointment with bureaucratic rationality and its replacement of charismatic authority. Schmitt's political theology is thus an expression of a political 'disenchantment' experienced in the modern secular world. However, it is more than simply a diagnosis of a problem. It is also an attempt to solve the crisis of political legitimacy and to restore transcendence and 'dignity' to politics by affirming an authoritarian and 'decisionistic' idea of sovereignty. If sovereignty is to become meaningful again in modernity – if it is not simply to be collapsed into the administrative state and legal order – it must be recognised as having the ultimate authority to make decisions. In particular, it must be able to decide in exceptional situations, in states of emergency (*Ausnahmezustand*), in which the normal constitutional order is suspended and the sovereign can act in an unconstrained, unlimited way. Thus we have Schmitt's infamous formulation: 'Sovereign is he who decides on the exception' (Schmitt, 2005: 5). However, the exception is not just a particular situation determined by the state, but is central to the very meaning of sovereignty, which for Schmitt is a 'borderline concept', relating to the 'outermost sphere' (ibid.). In other words, sovereignty, as a juristic concept, always inhabits the position of exception in relation to the norm – the normal legal order that it exceeds and, in exceeding it, also founds and determines. The exception can never be wholly accounted for by the norm, nor can it be seen as deriving from it. Yet, while the sovereign exception always goes beyond the law, it can never be considered apart from it either, in the sense that it only has meaning in relation to the norm it transgresses.

This paradoxical logic emerges as part of Schmitt's critique of liberal constitutionalism, which sought to rein in the sovereign exception through the rule of law – and, more specifically, in his debate with the neo-Kantian positive legal theorist Hans Kelsen, who sought to identify the state with the law and developed a theory of positive law as wholly derived from a self-contained, self-referential series of norms with nothing outside it (see Kelsen, 1967). The problem with these theories, according to Schmitt, was that, in trying to rule out the exception, they failed to acknowledge the way in which legal norms and rules actually presuppose an exterior that grounds them, constitutes their limit, and has the authority to apply them to specific situations – an authority to decide when and how a norm is applied. It is the sovereign exception that therefore guarantees the law: 'All law is "situational law". The sovereign produces and guarantees the situation in its totality' (Schmitt, 2005: 13). Moreover, unlike the norm, the exception embodies a certain contingency and vitality and should therefore be seen as prevailing over the rule:

> The exception is more interesting than the rule. The rule proves nothing; the exception proves everything. It confirms

not only the rule but also its existence, which derives only from the exception. In the exception the power of real life breaks through the crust of a mechanism that has become torpid by repetition. (Ibid., 15)

This idea of the exception is not only a way of restoring the state to its position of authority – the authority to make absolute decisions outside the law – but also a way of giving it back its 'personality'. The sovereign is not simply the administrative state governed by norms and rules, but a figure endowed with life who can act in the absence of rules. It is only an exceptional figure of this kind that has the capacity for general representation, who can provide a genuine point of transcendence and legitimacy, and whose absolute decision can unite and galvanise a social order. Do we not see the same fantasies invested today in the figure of the 'great decider', the political leader who violates the norms, who denounces the torpidity of the rule-governed liberal order, who embodies – in his erratic behaviour, in his unpredictability – a certain excess of life at the limits of the law?

The Sovereign Counterrevolution

My claim here is that the sovereign state of exception is a politico-theological weapon designed to neutralise the threat posed not so much by liberalism but by more radical forms of politics, especially anarchism. Curiously enough, the state of exception – the condition in which the rule of law is suspended – itself resembles a form of anarchy, perhaps what Hannah Arendt referred to as the 'anarchy of power' that characterised totalitarian regimes. However, Schmitt is quick to distinguish the exception from anarchy and chaos: order in the juristic sense still prevails, even if it is, he says ominously, 'not of the ordinary kind' (Schmitt, 2005: 12). This is a kind of artificially induced 'anarchy', designed to preserve rather than overthrow the existing order, or – as we saw in Schmitt's welcoming of the Nazi revolution – overthrowing it in order to preserve it.[4] To borrow the concept of 'immuni-sation' from the theorist Roberto Esposito (2011), the excep-tion might be seen as gesture in which, in order to protect oneself from a virus, one injects oneself with it so that the system's immune response is triggered. In the same way, to immunise itself against the threat of anarchy, the state sus-pends the rule of law and becomes 'anarchic'.

Schmitt's enmity towards anarchism is spoken through a series of conservative counterrevolutionary thinkers – de Maistre, de Bonald, and particularly Donoso Cortes – to whom the later sections of *Political Theology* are devoted. Cortes, writing, like Schmitt, in a time of political deca-dence in the wake of the 1848 revolutions, also claimed that sovereignty was necessarily absolutist and came to the conclusion that the only way of preserving the purity and sanctity of the sovereign decision in the wake of the final collapse of the old monarchical order was dictatorship. Like Schmitt, Cortes in his time is adrift in a world of atheism, materialism, liberalism and the dissolution of traditional morality and authority. He saw this in theological terms, as the battleground of a metaphysical struggle; he saw 'only the theology of the foe' (Schmitt, 2005: 62). Cortes had nothing but contempt for liberalism, seeing in it only the hypocrisy of the bourgeoisie and the inability to make decisions. Liberal politics was nothing but a debating chamber that intermi-nably postpones the decision, drowning it in endless delib-eration and equivocation. Rather, it was in revolutionary anarchism, especially Proudhon, that Cortes saw, and even admired, a true enemy, an enemy worthy of theological and political war. We are reminded here of Schmitt's definition of the enemy as *hostis* rather than *inimicus*: the enemy may not necessarily be hated – he may even be admired – but he is nevertheless recognised as the enemy with whom one is prepared to do battle (see Schmitt, 2007).[5] The anarchist, in his absolute rejection of God and the state, is the curious mirror image of the conservative: both recognise that the state is an absolutist concept, one to affirm it, the other to abolish it: 'To him [Cortes], every sovereignty acted as if it were infallible, every government was absolute – a sentence that the anarchist could pronounce verbatim, even if his intention was an entirely different one' (Schmitt, 2005: 55). Furthermore, this absolutism on both sides was based on their diagrammatically opposed understandings of human nature: for the conservative, man was inherently evil and corrupt, and therefore had to be reined in by a strong state; for the anarchist, man was inherently good and could therefore be trusted with freedom and self-government, whereas it was the sovereign who was corrupt and whose intervention corrupted the lives of men.

So, for Schmitt, as Bakunin before him recognised, we have a sort of religious war – or rather a political war, or a war over the very meaning and survival of politics, but one that is nevertheless cast in theological terms – between two kinds of 'extremisms' or 'absolutisms': on the one hand, a radical conservatism that affirms absolute sovereignty and a strong, authoritarian state; on the other, an atheistic revolutionary anarchism that seeks to overthrow the state in the name of materialism and the immanence of life. Such were the stakes in this politico-theological war, and such was the irreconcilability of its protagonists, that the anarchists would, in open rebellion against all authority, declare themselves on the side of Satan against God and the state (ibid., 64). These antagonistic positions, however, are united in their shared absolutism, something that leads, according to Schmitt, to paradoxical conclusions, particularly for the anarchist. Because the anarchist must absolutely reject the sovereign decision, as it interferes with the immanence of life,

> this antithesis forces him of course to decide against the decision; and this results in an odd paradox whereby Bakunin, the greatest anarchist of the nineteenth century, had become in theory the theologian of the antitheological and in practice the dictator of the antidictatorship. (Ibid., 66)

I will explore the meaning and aptness of Schmitt's curious charge against anarchism in a later chapter. It may well be that nineteenth-century anarchism, in its absolute hostility towards religion and in its veneration for the immanence of life, engaged in a certain metaphysics of its own and thus fell into a different kind of politico-theological bind. However, it is certainly the case that, for Schmitt, the struggle against anarchism is a theological struggle. This is emphasised in his text on Catholicism, where he once again envisages an absolute war with anarchism. Here, again, the target is the old enemy, Bakunin, depicted as a beserker, a barbarian from the Russian steppes, one who strikes with 'Scythian might' against religion and politics, theology and jurisprudence – against everything that Schmitt holds dear (Schmitt, 1996b: 36). The church has in the past stood on the side of counter-revolution in order to defend the idea and, indeed, the whole of Western European civilisation against the eastern barbarism of the Russian anarchist. Against such an implacable foe one must make a decision and choose a side: 'There is, nevertheless, a type of decision the church cannot avoid – a type of decision that must be taken in the present day, in concrete situations, in every generation' (ibid., 38). There is a sort of eternal metaphysical horizon of conflict that we are ever called upon to join. For Schmitt, the war between the church and anarchism is a politico-theological war; and it is by taking a side in this war, by making a political decision to enter the fray, that the church rediscovers its consistency as a political idea. The threat posed by Bakunin and by atheist anarchism thus acts as an *intensifier* of the political.

In Schmitt's concept of the political, it is the existential struggle against the enemy that turns religious organisations into political organisations and religious conflicts into political conflicts (see Schmitt, 2007: 36–7). And yet, as I have shown, his notion of the political has to rely, in turn, on a theological dimension in order to have consistency and intensity. In other words, the fact that the existential struggle that gives meaning to political life – which, as I have shown, is at its most intense when it confronts anarchism – has to be couched in theological terms, as a kind of apocalyptic war in which everything is at stake, shows that 'the political' relies upon a theological moment to give it shape. This suggests a deeper engagement between politics and theology than simply a series of 'structural analogies', as proposed in *Political Theology*. Indeed, as Heinrich Meier argues, the question of faith – faith in divine revelation – is absolutely central to Schmitt's theory of politics. Faith, with the obedience it commands, is what unites a political community – a community of believers against the Antichrist – and enjoins them to war and sacrifice. Authority, revelation and obedience are the key elements of Schmitt's theory of politics, and the political dimension that Schmitt sanctifies always carries theological meaning. As Meier (1998: 76) says in relation to Schmitt's thought: 'Man can be grasped wholly *politically* only because and only insofar as the political obeys a *theological* determination.'

Schmitt and Strauss: Political Theology and Political Philosophy

We must investigate further these ideas of faith, revelation and obedience, as they form the terrain of the debate between Carl Schmitt and Leo Strauss, a terrain upon which political theology might be more clearly distinguished from political theory. I have argued that Schmitt is a political thinker rather than a theologian. However, he is a political thinker of a very particular kind, one whose concept of politics is derived from theology and saturated with theological categories, modes of thinking and impulses – impulses that, as we have seen, are brought out into the open in the metaphysical struggle with anarchism.

The 'hidden dialogue' (see Meier, 1995) between Schmitt and Strauss can be found, most directly, in Strauss's critical reading of Schmitt's *The Concept of the Political* (*Der Begriff des Politischen*) – a reading to which Schmitt responded by making substantial revisions in the 1932 version of this text. In his 'Notes on Carl Schmitt', Strauss focuses on Schmitt's critique of liberalism and the liberal 'philosophy of culture', a critique that Strauss in many ways shares. Yet Schmitt's reliance on Hobbes, whom Strauss regards as an essentially liberal thinker, suggests that he is still caught within the horizons of liberalism, and thus 'his unliberal tendency is restrained by the still unvanquished "systematics of liberal thought"' (Strauss, in Schmitt, 2007: 122). Strauss's diagnosis of liberal secular modernity nevertheless bears some similarity to Schmitt's – that, in its all-encompassing rationalism and materialism, modernity simply reoccupies the place of religion, creating a new kind of 'faith', one that is actually hostile to the conditions of philosophy just as, for Schmitt, it was hostile to the conditions of politics. In other words, while it was once the orthodoxy of religion that presented a threat to philosophy, it is now the orthodoxy of reason itself (Strauss, in Meier, 2006: 141–80). Moreover, the special place and vocation of philosophy as the rational quest for truth is drowned out in the dissonance and nihilism of liberal modernity and eclipsed by the plurality of domains into which human life and activity is parcelled out – politics, economics, art, science, culture and so on. For Strauss and Schmitt, then, modernity makes transcendence difficult. Both thinkers try, in their own ways and for their own reasons, to come to terms with the relationship between theology and politics in the conditions of modern secularism, although they reach different conclusions. For Strauss, modernity has failed to solve what he calls the theologico-political problem – it has only repressed it. Modern bourgeois society is just as indifferent to the questions and claims of politics as it is to religion (Meier, 2006: 13).

But what is this original theologico-political predicament that, according to Strauss, has been overshadowed by modernity, and how does it relate to the vocation and status of philosophy? Theology and politics have both presented challenges to philosophy. There is a major tension between philosophy and theology, brought out by Spinoza's philosophical assault on religious orthodoxy. Strauss sees Spinoza's critique of religious orthodoxy, Jewish and Christian, in the *Tractatus theologico-politicus* as part of a liberal rejection of theology and as an attempt to secure a certain freedom for philosophising in an age of theological dogmatism (Strauss, 1982: 112). In trying to make philosophy independent of Scripture and free it from the constraints of religious orthodoxy, Spinoza claims that the true message of Scripture is beyond human understanding and that it is therefore impossible to derive from it a literal or dogmatic meaning that might be used to limit the philosopher's freedom. He also contests the authority of revelation on the grounds of reason. However, Strauss argues that Spinoza is ultimately unable to disprove revelation or demonstrate the non-existence of miracles. All he does is highlight the incompatibility between reason and revelation, philosophy and theology.

Philosophy and revelation are, according to Strauss, two incommensurable ways of thinking: while philosophy is a quest for truth, based on reason and free enquiry, revelation is based on faith; while philosophy is fundamentally sceptical and demands demonstrations and proofs, revelation is based on belief and obedience to God's authority. Because of their incompatibility, philosophy and revelation must try to disprove each other. In particular, because the Bible presents itself as the only form of authority and because its claims are so radically incompatible with the philosophical mode of enquiry, philosophy *must* refute revelation. However, and this is the key thing, philosophy *cannot* refute revelation (Strauss, in Meier, 2006: 150). Reason simply cannot dislodge faith. By the same token, revelation cannot refute philosophy either, even though it is equally compelled to do so. If the theologian, for instance, points out the moral laxity of philosophy, the philosopher might respond by asking for proof that truth is necessarily concerned with morality; if the theologian accuses the philosopher of pride, the philosopher might respond by asking who is more proud, 'he who says that his personal fate is of concern to the cause of the universe, or he who humbly admits that his fate is of no concern whatever to anyone but to himself and his few friends' (Strauss, in Meier, 2006: 163).

What is the point of this dialogue of the deaf between philosophy and revelation that Strauss sets up? Despite their incompatibility, theology imposes an invaluable test on philosophy, forcing it to question its own limits and consistency (Meier, 2006: 20). Strauss believes that being reminded of the confrontation with revelation might restore philosophy's honour by recalling its original, premodern vocation. So, for Strauss, philosophy, if it can be redeemed in modernity – in which it has become compartmentalised, professionalised and relativised, divided from science and made subordinate to it – has to be seen as an alternative to both biblical faith and modern unbelief (Strauss, in Meier, 2006: 143). It is only through the encounter with theology and in the rediscovery of its origins that philosophy can become once again an enquiry about truth and about how one should live. It is only by submitting to the test of theology that philosophy can genuinely come to terms with the theologico-political problem.

Where does this leave *political* philosophy? The fate of Socrates perhaps best symbolises the ancient tension between the demands of philosophy – with its eternal question of 'how should I live?' – and the demands of the political community. The philosopher's quest for truth is seen as more important than the demands of collective political life, which makes it always subversive (Strauss, in Meier, 2006: 146). We cannot imagine Schmitt – who demands of the individual total obedience to the political community – as having much sympathy for the philosopher. And, indeed, this goes to the heart of the difference between political philosophy and political theology. For Strauss, political philosophy begins with the trial and conviction of Socrates. It was the quarrel between the obligations of the polis and the vocation of the philosopher that would lead to a radical questioning of the beliefs and opinions of the day and gave rise to a certain way of enquiring about the nature of politics that we find exemplified in Plato and Aristotle. Political philosophy, for Strauss, is a branch of philosophy and is guided by the same quest for truth, wisdom and universal knowledge (Strauss, 1957:

343–68). Political philosophy thus enquires after the good, the good life and the best type of regime and believes that political activity should be oriented towards this eternal goal. It pits *knowledge* of political matters against mere *opinion*, and measures them against universal standards of truth and justice. Unlike modern positivist political science, which aims to be 'value-free', political philosophy, at least in its classical form, is able to provide answers to the central question 'What is political?' (ibid., 351).

Schmitt, too, is fundamentally concerned with answering this question. However, as we have seen, he approaches it in a radically different way, through political theology. Unlike political philosophy, which is based on free rational enquiry about how one should live, and thus requires reflection and self-examination, political theology is based on divine revelation and obedience to authority – the authority of both the heavenly and the worldly sovereign. As Meier (2006: 84) defines it, political theology is 'a political theory, political doctrine, or a political position for which, on the self-understanding of the political theologian, divine revelation is the supreme authority and the ultimate ground'. Because it can only be grounded in faith and obedience to the truth of revelation, it is radically inhospitable to a rational justification of one's way of life. As I have argued, Schmitt can be seen as a political theologian in this precise sense. His 'sociology' of juridical and political concepts, which claims to only display 'analogies' with theology, is actually steeped in theological ideas of faith, revelation, sacrifice and unquestioning obedience, where divine authority is simply mapped onto political authority. We cannot imagine anything more incompatible with political philosophy. So, while both Schmitt and Strauss are concerned with defining what is political 'today' at a time when, under the brunt of nihilism and positivism, this question has become utterly obscure, they approach it in entirely opposed ways. While both thinkers – who might be described as 'conservative', each in his own way – eschew liberal pluralism in search of a place of transcendence and legitimacy, one turns to political authoritarianism and the sovereign decision, while the other returns to the ancient search for truth.

To what extent can political philosophy be an antidote to political theology? Surely the philosophical quest for truth and the best form of life is preferable to an authoritarian understanding of politics founded on faith and obedience; surely, a process of rational and free enquiry into the conditions of our collective existence is preferable to the unilateral sovereign decision that closes off all further investigation. The open-ended search for truth in politics – whatever that might be – is undoubtedly more legitimate than blind faith and obedience. However – and here we return to the doubts expressed by Strauss himself – it is by no means certain that reason alone can overturn faith and obedience, especially in the field of politics. Perhaps political philosophy as Strauss conceives of it, as the detached contemplation of eternal truths, lacks the intensity and political commitment – that which was characteristic of Bakunin's fiery anarchism, for instance – to adequately contend with political theology. This is a question I shall return to.

The Theological Impossibility of Political Theology

Another way of confronting political theology is to try to refute it, not on philosophical grounds, but on theological grounds. This was precisely the aim of the theologian and Catholic convert Erik Peterson, a contemporary of Schmitt's, who in his 1935 essay 'Monotheism as a Political Problem' sought to demonstrate the theological illegitimacy of political theology. Here he shows that any kind of analogy between earthly and divine sovereignty, such as Schmitt draws, is contradicted by Christian theology. In particular, the idea of the triune God in the Trinitarian doctrine of Gregory of Nazianzus in the fourth century AD contradicted the idea of a divine monarchy, at least one that could be translated into earthly terms. Therefore the idea of a single sovereign ruler simply had no basis in theology. Moreover, the attempt within Christianity to use theological ideas to justify certain political formations – as, for instance, Bishop Eusebius of Caesarea, the 'court theologian of Constantine', tried to do with respect to the Roman Empire in the fourth century – could not be accepted on the basis of Christian eschatology. In this way, Peterson sought to make political theology impossible by pointing out the illegitimacy of translating theological concepts into political concepts (see Peterson, 2011: 68–105). This was a critique aimed directly at the politico-theological undertakings of his old friend, Carl Schmitt.[6] The parallel Schmitt drew between metaphysical and political concepts – which depended on the idea of divine monarchy – was a Hellenistic translation of Jewish monotheism, and was thus more pagan than Christian: 'Only on the basis of Judaism and paganism can such a thing as "political theology" exist' (Peterson, 2011: 105).

How did Schmitt respond to this wounding from the 'Parthian arrow' fired by his once friend, Peterson, so many years before? In his last book – *Political Theology II: The Myth of the Closure of Any Political Theology*, published in 1970 – Schmitt accused Peterson of a fundamental misunderstanding of political theology. Peterson's critique of monotheism and its serving as the theological basis for monarchy applied only to the monarch as an individual person, not to the idea of sovereignty as a *juridical* person, which is what Schmitt is principally interested in. More than this, when the theologian claims that political monotheism is theologically brought to an end, he is making a *political* claim – he demands *authority over power* – and, thus, is engaging in a political theology of his own: 'This claim becomes politically more intense along with the degree to which theological authority claims to supersede political power' (Schmitt, 2008: 113). Just as in the relation of enmity, the conflict between theology and politics becomes intensified and therefore *politicised*: 'If the theologian insists on his theological decision, then he has decided on a political question theologically and has claimed for himself a kind of political competence' (ibid., 113). It seems that the theologian, in his attempts to distance theology from politics, finds himself caught up in the politico-theological nexus he seeks to avoid.

Schmitt, as a *political* theologian, wants to pull theology onto a political terrain. Indeed, he wants to show that, even within theology itself, insofar as it was influenced by the old Gnostic dualist doctrine, there is an immanent *stasis* or conflict, which can become politicised (ibid., 126). There can be no pure theology pitted against an impure politics. The moment one tries to do this one finds oneself back within the horizon of politics one tried to escape from. Is it the case, then, that one cannot contest political theology from the position of theology alone? Perhaps, just as political theology necessarily moves within a theological horizon – more than Schmitt himself acknowledges – theology necessarily moves within a political horizon, despite its protestations of steering clear of politics. However, I would argue here that political theology can only ever be the affirmation and sacralisation of political sovereignty, and therefore there can be no such thing as a 'radical political theology'.[7] This does not mean, of course, that there cannot be a radical *theology*, or that theology cannot play a more public role and embrace emancipatory causes. Schmitt himself mentions two radical theologians, the Catholic Johann Baptist Metz and the Protestant Jürgen Moltmann, both of whom advocated a more public and political role for the church. Indeed, for these two, the only way in which theology could redeem itself 'after Auschwitz', and especially after the Vatican's 'Concordat' with the Nazi regime and its shameful silence on Nazi atrocities, was to engage in a critique of power. To this end, Metz's 'liberation theology' drew on the resources of Marxist theory and the Frankfurt School (see Metz, 1998).[8] Moltmann (1999: 5) argued that theology should be on the side of human rights, freedom, and even environmental liberation. Theology therefore had a public role to play. However, this does not make it political theology, at least not in the way I have defined it. While Schmitt might agree with the deprivatisation of religion urged by Moltmann and with the idea that theology and the church should take a public, political form once again, we cannot imagine, in this new role for theology, political commitments any more radically opposed to those of Schmitt.

Different Readings of the Apocalypse: Taubes and Schmitt

I will consider the efficacy of this new theology in a later chapter, but it is important at this stage to investigate where exactly one might locate within theology the resources and foundations for the radical critique of power. Here I turn to the Jewish philosopher Jacob Taubes, in whose thinking on St Paul we find an alternative, messianic horizon that allows a much more radical reading of theology than that countenanced by the 'apocalyptic prophet of the counterrevolution', Schmitt. Indeed, for Taubes, whose intellectual engagement and later correspondence with Schmitt began in 1948, both himself and Schmitt are apocalyptic thinkers, but Schmitt thinks 'from above', whereas he thinks 'from the bottom up' (Taubes, 2013: 13). We have seen already what thinking the apocalypse 'from above' means for Schmitt – the counterrevolution, instigated by the sovereign exception, designed to preserve the state order from the threat of revolution, and yet that ultimately authorised the Nazi apocalypse that ended up destroying the German state. So how should we understand the alternative apocalypse from below that Taubes invokes? Revolutions, in their destruction of the existing order, in their overturning of hierarchies, are of course apocalyptic events. Is there a deeper theological basis for revolutionary politics?

In his reading of St Paul's Epistle to the Romans – an address to the Jewish Christian congregations in Rome (ca AD 57–8) – Taubes finds an eschatological register that operates as a direct revolutionary counterpoint to Schmitt's counterrevolutionary political theology. Schmitt's political theology, as we have seen, tries to prevent the revolution from occurring, even if it has to stimulate a certain form of legal anarchy – the state of emergency – in order to capture

and contain within the order of power the real anarchy of
the revolution. In theological terms, the sovereign plays the
role of the *katechon* – the 'witholding power' that prevents
the coming of the Antichrist, the event that precedes the
Apocalypse and the arrival of the Messiah. Schmitt is one
who, in Taubes's words, 'prays for the preservation of the
state, since if, God forbid, it doesn't remain, chaos breaks
loose, or even worse, the Kingdom of God!' (Taubes, 2003:
69–70). We find the recurring theme of a theological and
political order, whose historical collapse in modernity risks
hastening the apocalypse – which Schmitt identifies with the
nihilism of liberal secular modernity – as well as precipitates
the search for a new order. However, Taubes's interpretation
of Paul offers a more revolutionary perspective. Not only is
Romans a declaration of war against the authority of Caesar
– Christ is declared emperor in his place; it is also the reg-
istering of an eschatological horizon, in which the end of
world and the coming of the Messiah are imminent and the
transience and unimportance of this-worldly political power
becomes apparent. For Paul, the coming of the Messiah who
will redeem the world is concomitant with the destruction
of the Roman Empire. In Taubes' hands, Paul's messianism
is a kind of revolutionary state of exception in which the
order of power crumbles away. This is in direct contrast and
opposition to Schmitt's conservative political theology, in
which the order of power is preserved at all costs.

We can also interpret this revolutionary theology as a
revolution *against* political theology, a way of overcoming,
once and for all, the nexus between theology and politics.
In this apocalyptic revolutionary horizon – which I have only
briefly sketched here – the structural apparatus that both
differentiates and binds together theology and politics will
be transcended, the two poles collapsing and disappearing
into each other. For Taubes (2010: 232),

> the secret nexus between the two realms is established by
> the concept of power. Only when the universal principle of
> power is overruled will the unity of theology and political

theory be superseded. A critique of the theological element in political theory rests ultimately on a critique of the principle of power itself.

One of the concerns of this chapter was to understand the relationship between political theology and political theory (or philosophy). As I have shown, while these are distinct ways of thinking – one based on revelation, faith and obedience, the other based on free and rational enquiry – they are nevertheless intertwined, one posing fundamental questions for the other. If political theory is to find convincing answers to these questions, it must find ways around the politico-theological problem. However, this is not a matter of extricating politics from theology – as we have seen, things are not quite so simple. Rather it is a matter of understanding, coming to terms with, and thinking beyond the problem of power that generates the continual oscillation between the political and the theological.

2

Max Stirner and the Ghosts of the Secular Modern

If the problem of political theology arises with secularism, we need to understand how the secular condition acts as the foundation and impetus for a theological framing of political concepts. In other words, what is it about modern secularism that uncannily resembles the theological world it displaced? It is here that I turn to the nineteenth-century German philosopher Max Stirner. As we have seen already, anarchists often make the best diagnosticians of the problem of political theology, and this is no less true of the individualist anarchist Stirner, who shared with Bakunin an extreme hostility to state authority. However, Stirner's assault on political theology and religious idealism also turns against the atheist–humanist and materialist discourses and moral and rational norms that underpinned revolutionary politics in the modern era. Here he detects a similar Christianising impulse, in secular–atheist form. Indeed, Stirner shows the whole of secular modernity to be haunted by the spectres of religion it had believed itself to be rid of. It was only through a complete overhaul of our categories of thought and politics that these spectres could be exorcised from our midst. Such was the radical nature of Stirner's diagnosis of secularism, that Schmitt recognised in him a strange affinity and brotherhood. As Schmitt wrote in his reflections as a prisoner in an Allied internment camp after the Second World War, Stirner's ghost was the only one to visit him in his captivity (see Schmitt, 2017).

Like Schmitt, then, Stirner's thought may be seen as a response to the incomplete nature of modern secularism. However, whereas Schmitt seeks to fill the gap left by the collapse of religious authority with new figures of the transcendent in the form of absolute sovereignty, Stirner wants to banish the transcendent once and for all. Both recognise that secular modernity bears a theological trace – the absent presence of religion. However, Schmitt seeks within this new sources of political legitimacy, while Stirner sees it as a precondition for the radical overcoming of all political power and authority and the destruction of its religious 'spirit'. In other words, while both recognise the politico-theological problem, they draw from it radically opposed conclusions. For Schmitt, secular modernity means the lack of a place of transcendence, a situation to be remedied by calling upon theological resources to establish a new point of legitimacy. For Stirner, it means the stubborn persistence of religion in the very structures of secular modernity. While, for Schmitt, modern liberal secularism is nihilism, for Stirner, modern liberal secularism is not 'nihilistic' enough. However, it would be wrong to see Stirner as insisting simply on greater secularisation. Secularism is simply a repression of the problem of religion; in displacing religion – in formally separating church from state and putting man in the place of God – it has simply incorporated religious authority into its structures and discourses, giving Christianity new life. Secular humanism can thus be seen as the fulfilment, rather than the overcoming, of religion. Instead, we must desacralise the sacred, not in order to make the profane sacred – which falls into the same trap – but to finally grasp the capacity for a 'this-worldly' life. Stirner's contribution to the politico-theological debate lies, I argue, in freeing our subjectivity from the fixed forms of identification determined by religious idealism and in showing how we might live in this world rather than in the next.

Hegel's Religion of the State

As one of the lesser known Young Hegelian philosophers, Stirner has generally received scant attention from contemporary political theory. He is best known for the theoretical controversy over his critique of idealism and his subsequent repudiation by Marx and Engels in *The German Ideology*. However, Stirner's version of the secularisation hypothesis and his critique of political theology emerge largely in reaction to Hegel's philosophy. In his main work, *The Ego and Its Own* (*Der Einzige und sein Eigentum*, first published in 1844), Stirner characterises Hegel as a 'Lutheran' because he 'was completely successful in carrying the idea through everything' (Stirner, 1995: 85). Hegel's idealism was simply a hangover from Christianity. This 'idea', what Hegel called *Geist* or 'spirit', referred to the progressive development of the mind from sensuous immediacy and particular consciousness to the universal 'absolute idea' or absolute knowledge. This was also a dialectical process that would be borne out historically in the march of 'world spirit' (*Weltgeist*) through different phases of development, culminating in the liberal bourgeois state. In Hegel's narrative of the universal idea, the spirit of Christianity is essentially transposed and elevated into the modern secular state. The eschatological story of salvation inherent in Christianity is central to the idea of dialectical reconciliation: Hegel's 'cunning of reason', which drives historical events towards this state of fulfilment, is akin to divine providence. Moreover, Christianity provides the ethical substance for the liberal state, which formally separates itself from the church and, in so doing, becomes the secular incarnation of the universal Christian idea. For Hegel (2001a: 353) then, the unfolding of the spirit of reason throughout the world is simply the unfolding of religion, and its culmination in the secular state is the realisation of the kingdom of God on earth.

Hegel thus reveals himself as a political theologian par excellence. While Schmitt derives his decisionist theory of the sovereign from the public *auctoritas* of the Catholic

Church and Hegel derives his constitutional monarchic state from the inner spirit of Protestantism, both see the state as a secular expression of theological authority and legitimacy. However, the Hegelian state is not a theocracy. Rather, it is the incorporation of the Christian religion into the universal secular state, a 'sublation' (*Aufhebung*) whereby Christianity is both elevated and transcended. Thus, in separating itself from the church and establishing its pre-eminence over religion, the state itself becomes divine: 'We must hence honour the state as the divine on earth.' For Hegel, then, the state is an ethical community, a living unity that contains the 'absolute content of religion' (ibid., 210). It may be seen as the secular embodiment of God on earth:

> The state is the march of God in the world; its ground or cause is the power of reason realizing itself as will. When thinking of the idea of the state, we must not have in our mind any particular state, or particular institution, but must rather contemplate the idea, this actual God, by itself. (Ibid., 197)

It is this new religion of the state that Stirner strongly objects to. Indeed, it is really no different from the old, just better disguised and more perfidious. If, for Hegel, the state is the actualisation of freedom, Stirner sees it as the antithesis of freedom. There is a fundamental incompatibility between individual freedom and state authority, even in the constitutional state, which supposedly protects rights and freedoms. The egoist is therefore the 'deadly enemy of the state' (Stirner, 1995: 227). Yet the fundamental hostility of the state to self-interest is simply an aspect of a more general tendency in idealist philosophy to subordinate the concrete reality and particularity of the individual to an abstract universal idea. As Hegel (2011: 148) says, '[t]he unending drive of thinking is to transpose what is real into ourselves as something that is universal and ideal. What human beings are as real they must be as ideal.' In this theologically inspired philosophy, the concrete individual is sacrificed on the altar of the ideal.

Stirner's critique of Hegel here reflects the anarchist rejection of idealism that we found in Bakunin: idealism, with its abstraction of reality into supernatural, metaphysical concepts, is always the ideology of power.

Stirner opposes Hegel's idealist philosophy with a counterdialectic – an alternative account of mankind's development that subverts the Hegelian dialectic and culminates not in the rational state as the fulfilment of the universal ideal, but rather in the triumphant egoist who embodies the destruction of the state and the desecration all universal ideals. Stirner's tripartite account of world history is divided into the time of the ancients, representing realism; the time of the moderns, representing idealism; and the future, which is the time of egoism. Paralleling Hegel's account of how the sensuous immediacy of the earliest stages of consciousness gradually developed into a more universal idea, Stirner shows how the ancients' relationship to the mundane world was superseded by Stoic philosophers and ascetic Christians – who sought to detach themselves from worldly concerns and pursue entirely spiritual goals – and later by the modern idealists, who sought the 'spirit' in everything. The Protestant Reformation is the event that truly entrenches the 'spirit' into daily life and into the hearts of individuals, enjoining them to despise and turn away from everything corporeal and particular (Stirner, 1995: 28). The relentless search for the 'truth' of the world that characterises modernity encourages us eventually to look behind God for a deeper and more fundamental truth, a higher and more universal ideal. Yet, as Stirner will show, the project of humanism – which seeks to replace God with 'man' – is simply a continuation of Christianity; nothing but 'the extremest efforts of "theology", that is, theological insurrections' (ibid., 30).

Stirner refers to us moderns as 'the possessed'. We are utterly haunted by spirit – whether an overtly religious desire or a secular desire for other ideals, like morality and rationality. We zealously persecute everything that is non-sacred, that does not live up to universal ideals, and we excoriate ourselves for the corporeal, sensual remainder within us that continually evades spiritual purification. We are consumed by the search for truth, for the essential truth behind appearances – and it is here that we not only deceive ourselves but reveal our genuine religiosity. Moral conviction, for Stirner, is no different from religious conviction and is adhered to just as dogmatically: 'This moral *faith* is deeply rooted in his breast. Much as he rages against pious Christians, he himself has remained thoroughly a Christian, namely a *moral* Christian. Christianity holds him a prisoner, and a prisoner under *faith*' (ibid., 45).

We can see how Stirner's account of the progress of the idea not only opposes Hegel's – in the sense that the idea, which Hegel associates with the development of freedom, becomes for Stirner an absolute tyranny – but also directly contradicts Schmitt's diagnosis of modern secularism. Unlike for Schmitt, modernity, for Stirner, is not characterised by nihilistic drift, moral relativism and the absence of transcendent ideas, but quite the contrary: we live in a world enthralled to the sacred and the transcendent. Does Stirner's description of the haunted world of modernity still resonate with our experience today? It would seem that, on the surface, things could not be more different. In an age characterised by the dissolution of traditional moral values and grand narratives, we are no longer possessed by a universal rational and moral idea in the manner Stirner described. At the same, are we not in the grip of other kinds of delusions, whether in the form of irrational and obscurantist religious beliefs – which seem to have returned in our secular modernity – or in the fixation on certain identities, whether national, cultural, political, sexual, gender, which we adhere to with a different kind of religious conviction? I will have more to say about this later, as I think Stirner's philosophy of egoism is an antidote to any politics of identity. However, just as in Stirner's time, which was full of pious priests of all kinds, promulgating the new rational religion of humanism, so too in our time we are surrounded by antagonistic communities of secular priests, signalling their virtue and piety with a new kind of religious fervour.

Feuerbach's 'Theological Insurrection'

I will turn later to the third, 'egoistic' stage of Stirner's counterdialectic. But we must first look more closely at the new
religion of humanism and its politico-theological implications. Who were the new secular priests of Stirner's time?
One such 'priest' was fellow Young Hegelian Ludwig Feuerbach. In his work *The Essence of Christianity*, Feuerbach
claimed that religion was alienating because it meant that
man abdicated his own qualities and powers, abandoning
them to the abstract, transcendent figure of God. In doing
so, man displaced and alienated his own essential nature, his
'species being'. While the human being should be the single
criterion for truth, love and virtue, these characteristics are
now the property of an abstract being, who becomes the sole
criterion for them: 'Religion is the disuniting of man from
himself; he sets God before him as the antithesis of himself...
God is the infinite, man the finite being; God is perfect, man
imperfect; God eternal, man temporal; God almighty, man
weak; God holy, man sinful' (Feuerbach, 1957: 1). The
project of humanism, then, as the overcoming of mankind's
alienation, is to reclaim these externalised qualities as our
own. Feuerbach's intention was to make the *human* the
divine, the *finite* the infinite.

However, Stirner saw in this humanist project simply the
substitution of one form of religious alienation and idealism
for another. In seeking to replace God with man, in showing
that qualities we attribute to God are really those of man,
Feuerbach had succeeded not in liberating us from the religious illusion, but only in reaffirming it. Rather than overthrowing the categories of religious authority and alienation
– the religious place of transcendence – Feuerbach has
inverted the terms, thus embarking on a chain of substitutions: man for God, morality and rationality for theology,
human essence for spirit. The problem is that, when God
becomes man, man himself becomes God, capturing and
preserving the category of the infinite. Man becomes the
ultimate religious illusion and an expression of a new kind

of divine power. Feuerbach's secular emancipation is therefore incomplete and leads us back into the trap of religious belief. In modernity, we come to believe in 'man' and 'humanity' in the same way in which we believed in God; humanism is simply a new form of religious faith. Like God, the 'essence of man' is a superstitious ideal that oppresses the individual: '*I* am neither God nor *man*, neither the supreme essence nor my essence, and therefore it is all one in the main whether I think of the essence as in me or outside me' (Stirner, 1995: 34). For Stirner, the 'I', the ego, cannot be reduced to human essence. Yet, in making the 'essence' of man sacred, Feuerbach has created a new form of alienation, in which the individual ego is subordinated to the universal figure of 'man' in exactly the same way in which humanity was once subordinated to the universal figure of God. For Stirner, then, '"Man" is the God of today, and fear of man has taken the place of the old fear of God' (ibid., 165). Feuerbach was the high priest of the new human religion, which, for Stirner, is 'only the last metamorphosis of the Christian religion' (ibid., 158).

Spooks

Along with Hegelian idealism, Feuerbach's theological insurrection has contributed, according to Stirner, to the creation of a modern secular world haunted by the legacy of religion. We are surrounded by spooks, ghosts, ideological abstractions, figments of our imagination that dominate our consciousness. 'Man,' declares Stirner, 'your head is haunted... You imagine great things, and depict to yourself a whole world of gods that has an existence for you, a spirit-realm to which you suppose yourself to be called, an ideal that beckons to you' (Stirner, 1995: 43). We are plagued by what Stirner calls 'fixed ideas' – moral and rational absolutes, universal ideals, and identities that we cling on to. Fixed ideas have become the new place of the sacred and transcendent in secular modernity. As we have seen, the idea of essence, an essential truth to be sought behind the veil of appearances, is one such conviction – a belief that makes the whole world ghostly and immaterial:

> Look out near or far, a ghostly world surrounds you every-where, you are always having 'apparitions' or visions. Every-thing that appears to you is only the phantasm of an indwelling spirit, is a 'ghostly apparition'; the world to you is only a 'world of appearances', behind which the spirit walks. (Ibid., 36)

Fixed ideas not only imprison us within general moral and rational precepts that we are obliged to follow and conform to, but also abstract from the reality of the world and destroy the particularity of our existence. Fixed ideas make the world sacred and drown out the profane:

> But around the altar rise the arches of a church, and its walls keep moving further and further out. What they enclose is sacred... Shrieking with the hunger that devours you, you wander round about these walls in search of the little that is profane, and the circles of your course keep growing more and more extended. (Ibid., 89)

Stirner describes a world that has become a giant and expanding church that seeks to make everything sacred, eclipsing the possibilities of a profane worldly life.

Liberalism as Political Theology

As part of Stirner's critical diagnosis of modernity, he unmasks the theological impulses of secular politics. Central to this is liberalism, which he regards as a politico-theolog-ical apparatus, a kind of sacrificial machine, which, so far from freeing the individual, aims at the elimination of all singularity and uniqueness in the name of universal ideals. Liberalism, or what Stirner calls 'political liberalism', emerges with the development of the modern state. After the fall of the old monarchical order, a new locus of sovereignty comes into being, exemplified by the secular liberal state. Here

Stirner has in mind Hegel's constitutional state. However, behind the liberal bourgeois order there is a theological dimension that remains absolutist and that, in the guise of greater equality and liberty, ends up subordinating the individual to the divine power of the state. In freeing the individual from the arbitrary and despotic power of absolute monarchs, it ends up binding the individual much more closely and directly to the state order, cutting out the complex social relationships that once mediated the individual's interactions with the state. Thus,

> Political liberty means that the polis, the state is free; freedom of religion that religion is free, as freedom of conscience signifies that conscience is free; not therefore that I am free of the state, from religion, from conscience, or that I am *rid* of them. It does not mean my liberty, but the liberty of a power that rules and subjugates me. (Stirner, 1995: 96)

Under liberalism, all individuals become, as it were, political Protestants who enter into an immediate and intimate relationship with their new God, the state. Just as Marx contended that religious liberty meant only that religion was free to further alienate the individual in civil society, so Stirner argues that political liberty means only that the state is free to further dominate the individual. Furthermore, liberal notions of rights and equality only subject the individual to abstractions rather than enhancing his freedom. Equality of rights means only that 'the state has no regard for my person, that to it I, like every other, am only a man' (ibid., 93). Rights are granted, through the state, to man, a general abstraction, not to the individual. There is nothing wrong with equality as such; it is just that, through its embodiment in the liberal state, the individual is reduced to a fictional commonality that takes an institutionalised form. The dominant mode of subjectivity within this political order is the 'citizen', a category based on obedience and allegiance to the state.

Liberalism, for Stirner, can also take other forms, which develop beyond political liberalism. What Stirner calls 'social liberalism', or what we might think of as socialism, is a discourse that claims that the principle of equality be extended beyond the political to the social and economic domain – something that can only be achieved through the abolition of private property, which is seen as an alienating and depersonalising relation. However, according to Stirner, the subordination of property to the community means a further restriction of individual egoism and autonomy and, indeed, a coercive assimilation of the individual into a fictive collective body, society. Society thus replaces the state as the altar upon which the individual is sacrificed. For Stirner, society or community is another kind of religious illusion, a *corpus mysticum* or sacred body: 'Like the "nation" of the politicians, it will turn out to be nothing but a "spirit", its body only semblance' (ibid., 105). The third and final articulation of the dialectic of liberalism is humanist republicanism, or what Stirner calls 'humane liberalism' – and here he is referring to the thought of fellow Young Hegelian Bruno Bauer. In this discourse, which seeks a final reconciliation of the individual with humanity, all individual difference and singularity – all egoism, in other words – is transcended through identification with a universal idea of humanity, a common human essence that is believed to reside within everyone (ibid., 114). However, this, for Stirner, is the ultimate religious illusion. The humanist drive to overcome alienation – a drive that culminates in the emancipation of the human being from all particularities – only accomplishes the final and complete alienation of the individual.

However, this theological discourse of liberalism produces an excess, an irreducible remainder that it cannot entirely eliminate. This is what Stirner calls the 'un-man' (*Unmensch*): 'a man who does not correspond to the concept man, as the inhuman is something human which is not conformed to the concept of the human' (ibid., 159). The un-man is the other of man, the excess cast off by liberalism in its quest for the purity of the universal ideal. The un-man is everything that refuses to conform to the concept of man, that falls short of the required moral and rational norms of humanism and deviates from the calling of human essence. The un-man becomes the basis for a refusal of all forms of political and moral obligation, of the state and its laws, and even of society. It is precisely because these entities have no ego – no 'personality', as Schmitt would put it – that they cannot command our obedience and thus remain empty abstractions. So the un-man, in its refusal of all duty and obligation, is the counterpoint to liberalism: 'Liberalism as a whole has a deadly enemy, an invincible opposite, as God has the devil: by the side of man stands always the un-man, the individual, the egoist. State, society, humanity, do not master this devil' (ibid., 125). In terms similar to those of Bakunin's satanic struggle against political theology, Stirner envisages a struggle between the un-man, or the egoist, and the forces of society that seek to master and constrain him.

The Politics of Egoism

As an alternative to liberalism, Stirner proposes a form of egoism. As a philosophy of radical negativity, egoism seeks to clear the ontological ground of all abstractions and spooks, all figures of the transcendent. It performs an exorcism on our philosophical and political tradition. Egoism calls for the complete destruction of all fixed ideas, moral and rational universals, and the political concepts they animate. State, nation, society, community, citizenship are all profaned, brought down to the level of the individual egoist so that they can be appropriated and 'consumed'. For Stirner, the only possible solution to the problem of political theology is to desacralise the space of the sacred by bringing everything back to the ego as the only ontological reality. Stirner's egoism can be seen as part of his nominalist philosophy, which rejects all universal ideas and categories as meaningless. Rather meaning can only be determined from the particular perspective of the egoist, who has no regard for the sacred: 'The divine is God's concern; the human "man's". My concern is neither the divine nor the human, not the true, good, just, free, etc., but solely *what is mine* [das Meinige], and is not a general one, but is – *unique* [einzige], as I am unique' (Stirner, 1995: 7).

Who, then, is the egoist? While Stirner has often been interpreted as promoting a crude form of possessive individualism, the egoist or 'owner' is in no way reducible to the figure of the liberal individual. Indeed, the borders of the liberal subject are completely dissolved by ego, which should be thought of more as a singularity that is not predicated on any essential properties or characteristics. The ego, or as Stirner calls it, the 'unique one', should rather be thought of as a sort of self-creating void in subjectivity, a 'creative nothing' (ibid., 7), which is always determining its own predicates and is not guided by any general ideal or essence:

> I on my part start from a presupposition in presupposing myself; but my presupposition does not struggle for its perfection like 'Man struggling for his perfection', but only serves me to enjoy it and consume it... I do not presuppose myself, because I am every moment just positing or creating myself. (Ibid., 150)

In other words, the ego can never be expressed or exhausted within a particular concept or identity: 'They say of God, "names name thee not". That holds good of me: no concept expresses me, nothing that is designated as my essence exhausts me; they are only names' (ibid., 324). This is the closest Stirner comes to any kind of 'negative theology', where the meaning of God is approached by saying what God is not, rather than what he is.[1] However, instead of God being the unknowable, unnameable, beyond signification, it is the ego as the radical counterpoint to God. The ego is not so much a distinct subject but a deconstruction of all subjectivities. Put simply, the ego is not a 'fixed' idea or identity; indeed, it is the dissolution of the borders of all identities.

Understood in this way, Stirner's egoism might be seen as an antidote to 'identity politics', which is becoming, on both the left and the right, the dominant mode of political expression. The identity politics of the right, which organises itself around the 'fixed ideas' of nation, culture, race, religion and traditional gender roles, for instance, is confronted by an identity politics of the left, grouped around the recognition of ever more marginalised subject positions, particular ethnic, cultural and sexual minorities, and (trans)gender identities. In both cases, the identity being promoted is associated with a certain moral position, usually the position of the one who claims to be the victim of discrimination and non-recognition. One's identity becomes the only basis upon which one is authorised to speak and upon which other non-identifying voices are automatically delegitimised: 'As a white Christian male'; 'As a gay woman of colour'; 'As a trans-person' – and so on. From the perspective of Stirner's egoism, the problem with this sort of political discourse is its essentialism, whereby subjectivity is based on an essential meaning or category, and is thereby trapped within a fixed signifier. Even 'trans' identities, of which we have been hearing so much these days, do not necessarily break with the essentialism of identity but, on the contrary, insist even more fervently on the 'truth' of one's gender, to which one's physical body must be made to conform. Moreover, the problem with basing one's political position and moral attitude upon a certain identity is that politics is reduced to a series of representable categories, to be legally inscribed within the liberal state or catered for by the capitalist market; no identity must be excluded or denied recognition. However, this kind of politics has become a dead end. It is increasingly overladen with a moral piousness and censoriousness that only undermines its political efficacy and deteriorates into self-defeating cultural wars fought with the right. The challenge of Stirner's philosophy of egoism, it seems to me, is to create forms of politics that are not enthralled to, or dependent upon, particular identities, where politics becomes an activity, a mode of action and being in common in which one's 'identity' is of no interest whatsoever.

Stirner has no intention of outlining a political programme or prescribing any particular forms of politics – these are to be determined by egoists for themselves. However, he does provide us with some useful concepts. If, for instance, Stirner rejects all familiar political collectives as oppressive spooks, whether state, nation, community, society, political parties, is there any form of collective association that the egoist *would* countenance? Stirner's novel alternative is the paradoxical sounding 'union of egoists' – a sort of voluntary association that individuals enter into and leave freely. The 'union' is Stirner's alternative to the sovereign state – indeed, it implies the very dissolution of the state order (see ibid., 161). It is not a stable institution and it imposes on the individual member no binding obligations or duties. We cannot imagine anything more different or antithetical to Schmitt's idea of a political community under the authority of the sovereign, bound together by politico-theological faith and obedience. The union dissolves any pre-established political unity, especially any constituted by a sovereign place of transcendence. Or, put another way, there can be no sovereign exception with the union of egoists, because *all* are singular exceptions. Nor is the union a democracy as such. Indeed, Stirner is just as sceptical of the democratic state as he is of the authoritarian state: 'Every state is a despotism, be the despot one or many, or (as one is likely to imagine about a republic) if all be lords, that is, despotize over one another' (ibid., 175). Rather, we should think of the 'union of egoists' in terms of unstable, fluid sets of relations that emerge, mutate and dissolve rhizomatically. It can be seen as an experiment in autonomous modes of political action whose resistance to sovereign representation is designed to avoid getting caught up once again in transcendental, theological categories. As paradoxical and in some ways problematic a figure as it is, the 'union' might be seen as an alternative way of approaching the impossible question of the individual and the community and of forming a profane, 'this-worldly' way of being together that affirms the contingency and openness of the political as such.

Insurrection

Another of Stirner's useful concepts is the insurrection or 'uprising' (*Empörung*), a form of political action that is different from the revolution.

> Revolution and insurrection must not be looked upon as synonymous. The former consists in an overturning of conditions, of the established condition or *status*, the state or society, and is accordingly a *political* or *social* act; the latter has indeed for its unavoidable consequence a transformation of circumstances, yet does not start from it but from men's discontent with themselves, is not an armed rising but a rising of individuals, a getting up without regard to the *arrangements* that spring from it. The Revolution aimed at new arrangements; insurrection leads us no longer to *let* ourselves be arranged, but to arrange ourselves, and sets no glittering hopes on 'institutions'. It is not a fight against the established, since, if it prospers, the established collapses of itself; it is only a working forth of me out of the established. (Stirner, 1995: 279–80)

Whereas the revolution works to transform external social and political conditions, the insurrection is aimed at one's egoistic self-transformation. To engage in an insurrection means placing oneself *above* external conditions and constraints, whereupon these constraints simply disintegrate. It starts from the affirmation of the self, and the political consequences flow from this. The insurrection eschews the idea of an overarching project of emancipation or social transformation; freedom is not the end goal of the insurrection, but rather its starting point. It is a form of profane politics in the sense that it is not enthralled to a sovereign place of transcendence – in terms of either identifying with the institutions that fill this place or seeking to overthrow these institutions, only to erect new ones in their place. It turns away from this place of power altogether and affirms the self instead. Stirner's point is that, if political action does not become, as he puts it, 'my own cause', 'my own creation', then it risks becoming a sacred, abstracted cause alien to the individual, and to which the individual is ultimately sacrificed. So perhaps we can understand the insurrection as a way of thinking about revolutionary action in a non-theological, that is, *profane*, way.

Giorgio Agamben reflects on Stirner's idea of the insurrection in his work on St Paul, in the context of interpreting the enigmatic notion of *klēsis* or messianic vocation. As we have seen from the discussion in the last chapter, Taubes considers Paul's messianism as a revolt against the temporal power of Rome. However, rather than urging people to take up arms, Paul affirms a certain kind of 'nihilistic' indifference to this power, in the face of the imminent coming of the Messiah. This is particularly clear in the *hōs mē* (ὡς μή, 'as if not') passage from 1 Corinthians, where Paul encourages his followers to 'have as if one didn't have': 'The appointed time has grown short... From now on, let those who have wives be as though they had none... and those who mourn as though they were not mourning... and those who rejoice as though they were not rejoicing' (see Taubes, 2003: 53). This enigmatic passage is understood by Agamben as a profane refusal of vocation or, to be more precise, a vocation or calling that is at the same time a negation or the bringing to an end (in the sense of messianic time) of all vocations. While Stirner's profane egoistic politics would reject any association with messianism, there is a sense in which the insurrection involves a similar distancing of ourselves from our established identities or 'vocations', which otherwise sustain power. This indeed is the interpretation of Agamben, who suggests that Stirner's insurrection is one possible way of thinking about this refusal of vocation, an 'ethical anarchic' one, which proposes a radical disengagement from power rather than a revolution against it (Agamben, 2005b: 31–2).

I have suggested that in the ethical–political figures Stirner deploys, we find clues – and perhaps no more than clues – about the possibilities of living a profane life. At the very least, they can be seen as an attempt to think, live, associate and act in ways that escape the place of the sacred, which is the wellspring of political theology. As I have shown, to simply invert the terms of the politico-theological paradigm – to assert man in place of God, human essence and rationality in place of the sacred, or freedom against the state – is insufficient, as it simply reaffirms the place of transcendence and authority one opposes. Stirner therefore calls a halt to this chain of substitutions that only leaves us trapped in the nexus of power. At the heart of his egoistic philosophy there is a radical negativity that works against political theology and against the place of power that generates it. And perhaps we need to grasp this threshold if we are to move beyond the terrain of political theology.

3

God Is Unconscious

Psychoanalysis and Political Theology

What did Jacques Lacan mean when he said: 'The true formula for atheism is not *God is dead*... the true formula for atheism is *God is unconscious*' (Lacan, 1981: 59)? In this enigmatic formulation, psychoanalysis reveals the blind spot of secularism: secularism is premised not on the death of God, but on his repression and internalisation as a figure of the unconscious. The conceit of our secular age is to imagine that God is no longer with us, that he no longer shapes modern consciousness. Yet, just as Stirner showed in his critique of humanism and idealism, we have not yet succeeded in freeing ourselves from this spectre; we have only inverted the terms of religious authority and thus remain haunted by the categories of theological thought. More so, to imagine that we have finally transcended religion, that we have expelled God from our midst, as modern atheists are inclined to do, only confirms our continued enthralment with the place of the sacred and the transcendent once occupied by this figure. Modern atheists, in their cynical reason, may be the most devout believers. In an age characterised by the breakdown of symbolic authority – not only of religion but also of traditional forms of moral and political authority – we do not necessarily find ourselves more free, but subjected to new kinds of burdens and obligations. A psychoanalytic account of political theology, which draws on the theories of Freud and Lacan, can help us understand this problem and, possibly, find ways to counter it.

Freud and the Myth of the Primal Father

In his 1927 work *The Future of an Illusion*, Freud (1961b) argued that religion is a form of infantile wish fulfilment, an illusion that gives man succour and comfort by turning him away from reality. Religion develops out of the need to explain the uncontrollable forces of nature, to bestow meaning on an otherwise meaningless and futile existence, and to provide consolation in the face of death. The longing for God is really the longing for a protective and benevolent father who defends the helpless infant from the threats and privations of a hostile world. This is why, according to Freud, belief in God is marked by the same ambivalence as the child's relationship to the father, a mixture of love and fear (Freud, 1961b: 24). This is also why, despite the absurd and self-contradictory nature of religious doctrine, religious belief has proved so far to be intractable, even in the face of reasoned argument. We are reminded here of the impossible dialogue between theology and philosophy that Leo Strauss reflected upon. Unlike factual errors, religious illusions cannot so easily be disproven because they arise out of deep psychological needs, and their strength, according to Freud, lies in the wishes and desires they express. So, despite Freud's hope that the religious illusion would eventually give way to reason and science, and despite his conviction that religion was an unreliable foundation for the moral institutions of civilisation, he acknowledged the hold that religion, for the moment, had over the modern consciousness.

It is therefore important to investigate the reasons for the persistence of the religious illusion. For Freud, religion is a universal obsessional neurosis that arises out of an unresolved Oedipus complex. To explore this we must turn to one of Freud's key works, *Totem and Taboo* (Freud 2001;

originally published in 1913), in which he investigates the psychic origins of taboos, particularly the incest taboo, in 'primitive' totemic cultures. Prohibitions, especially against sexual promiscuity within the tribe, are symbolised by totems, totemic animals, which, Freud argues, are substitutes for the father – and it is the occasional and ritualistic killing and eating of what normally represents sacred animals that symbolise the emotionally ambivalent attitude, of both love and hatred, of the child towards the father that is the familiar dynamic of the Oedipal narrative. But how does this dynamic arise? This is where Freud proposes his famous hypothesis – a kind of cultural myth, which he also takes to be an evolutionary fact – of the primal horde. The horde is ruled by a jealous and violent father who enjoys unlimited and exclusive access to all the women of the group, thus depriving his sons of sexual enjoyment. The sons, who, as individuals, lived in fear of the father, one day banded together to overthrow, kill and devour him, thus putting an end to his patriarchal reign. However, so far from being henceforth free to enjoy the sexual access they had envied in their father, the brothers were overcome with remorse and forbade themselves what they had once coveted. The prohibition on sexual enjoyment enforced by the once hated primal father was now reaffirmed in the universal law against incest and articulated into forms of totemic authority and sacred rites. The murdered primal father thus lived on in the form of guilt and moral prohibition: 'The dead father became stronger than the living one had been ... What had up to then been prevented by his actual existence was thenceforward prohibited by the sons themselves' (Freud, 2001: 166).

Where does religion come into this? Freud is initially concerned with the origin of totemic religions, but these become the basis of all later religions, including monotheistic ones. The God of monotheism becomes the substitute for the father – no longer the ferocious primal father, but the benevolent, loving, omniscient father (ibid., 171). All religions can therefore be seen as ways of coming to terms with the guilt over this one great founding crime, a guilt that persists, phylogenetically, in the unconscious. Moreover, as totemic cultures gave way to more hierarchically organised societies, the power of the father-God increased. This figure came to occupy a place of absolute sacredness and transcendence within society, demanding veneration and sacrifices. This gave rise to more authoritarian and hierarchical political structures and the emergence of divine kings – absolute rulers who claimed their authority directly from God. Rather than the democratically organised band of brothers, we return to a more patriarchal society, once again under the control of an authoritarian ruler, but one whose power is now institutionalised in the form of a state. The symbolic power of the murdered primal father is thus intensified. As Freud says: 'It must be confessed that the revenge taken by the deposed and restored father was a harsh one: the dominance of authority was at its climax' (ibid., 174). We thus have the intertwining of religious and political authority that is central to political theology. Yet, as I have shown, the twist that Freud gives to the more familiar understanding of political theology is that before God there was the Father; that religious authority is itself a sublimation of an even older form of 'political' or prepolitical authority – the unlimited and exceptional power of the primal father, who lives on after his death, in symbolic form, both in organised religion and in the political institutions that later derive their legitimacy from it.

A similar politico-theological analysis is developed in Freud's last published work, *Moses and Monotheism* (Freud, 1939). Once again, there is the attempt to show that religion – particularly the monotheistic religions of Judaism and Christianity – are attempts to mediate and come to terms with collective guilt over an original crime, a traumatic event that led to the foundation of society. However, in this case, the murdered father is no longer the violent, sexually unrestrained primal father of the previous account but Moses, the founder of the Jewish people. As Freud speculates, however, Moses was actually an Egyptian and a follower of Pharaoh Akhenaton and his Aton religion. Moreover, it was this

monotheistic religion that Moses introduced to the Jewish
people. However, unable as they were to accept the imposi-
tion of such a spiritualised and austere religion, the Jews
rebelled and murdered their leader, later adopting in place
of the Aton religion a different god, Jahweh – a much more
simplistic and ferocious figure. Yet, and once again because
of guilt over the original crime, the Jews combined the earlier
Egyptian religion with their newly adopted religion. Jahweh
became simply the conduit for the earlier god he replaced.
Moreover, the figure of Moses as the father of their religion
was restored in the form of the Messiah, whose return would
bring their salvation.

The Primal Sovereign

Although the two father figures presented in Freud's narratives are quite different – the cold, rational Moses and
the sexually uninhibited and tyrannical primal father of
the horde – they are, both, embodiments of what Schmitt
would call the sovereign exception.[1] If we recall, for Schmitt,
the sovereign is defined by his right to decide on the exception, and thus stands outside the constraints of the normal
constitutional order. The sovereign is thus an expression of
both absolute authority and radical freedom and autonomy,
unrestricted by the laws that apply to everyone else. And
Schmitt's point is that it is precisely through this exceptional
position outside the law that the consistency and security of
the constitutional order is preserved; the exception verifies
the rule.

It is not too difficult to perceive a structural similarity
here with the original father figures of Freud's account. The
parallel is perhaps clearer with the primal father of *Totem
and Taboo*, an unrestrained, ferocious and violent sovereign who enjoys exclusive sexual access to the women and
tyrannises over his sons. However, the figure of Moses also
embodies a position of exceptionality – he is the foreigner,
the one who comes from outside and unilaterally imposes
a new and alien religion on his adopted people. The former

is a figure of transgressive enjoyment who rules through violence and intimidation, while the latter is a supreme law-giver who founds a people. Yet both are absolute sovereigns who occupy a position of exceptionality, exempting themselves from the rules and constraints they impose on others. However, the twist Freud gives to this story is that it is only through rebellion against the exceptional sovereign that the laws and rules of the political community are established. They arise as a means of coming to terms with the guilt of having betrayed him, of expiating the trauma – the psychic debt incurred with his murder. It is, in other words, only through the *removal* of the exceptional father that a political community can emerge and a system of laws can be established.

However, it would be wrong to draw from this apparent reversal of Schmitt's position any kind of democratic or egalitarian conclusions. We have seen how, in Freud's account, the murdered father – the exceptional sovereign – lives on, in symbolic form, in the political institutions established after his death and that, at the heart of all politics, there is an unresolved Oedipal complex, one that opens the possibility for more authoritarian forms of politics to emerge. In other words, the original act of rebellion and transgression, the murder of the original father figure, does not permanently institutionalise an egalitarian political community; it simply creates a permanent place of transcendence, a ground, watered with guilt, for future exceptional sovereigns to emerge. In fact liberal and democratic societies – founded on the myth of revolution against arbitrary authority – continue to be enthralled to this place of transcendence, and therefore remain permanently open to the dangers of the sovereign exception, as we see whenever governments threaten to restrict freedoms and rights in the name of security. The primal father becomes a strange double of the law: both abstracted into the symbolic authority of the law and embodying a kind of obscene, violent and excessive presence lurking behind it. At least 'primitive' man had the intelligence and foresight to confine the power of the dead father to profane objects, to totemic symbols and figures, which could be externalised and, on occasion, sacrificed as a kind of reassertion of the profane over the sacred. But later monotheistic religions, by abstracting this power into the figure of God as well as installing it within the psyche in the form of moral guilt, intensified it and made it permanent. The sovereign exception – that which both violates and supports the law – remains, but its presence is more fantasmatic, more a figure of the unconscious, and thus more pervasive and penetrating. So, in other words, the transgression of the authority of the primal father by no means puts an end to exceptional sovereignty but, on the contrary, only reinforces it. Even after his death, the exceptional sovereign lives on as a symbol of authority; the primal father becomes more powerful in death than he was in life.

In revealing the strange and uncanny afterlife of the murdered father, psychoanalysis opens up a new dimension to the politico-theological problem – that of the psyche and its interpenetration with both religion and politics.[2] Not only are religious ideas and structures of political authority internalised within the subject's psyche, where they inculcate guilt; these ideas and structures are themselves sublimations of unconscious processes, a way of externalising the effects of guilt and trauma. The logic of the sovereign exception lies at the threshold between the psyche and external structures of political and social authority. This is also the proper field of psychoanalytic investigation.

The Figure of the Leader

We can see this politico-theological dimension of exceptional sovereignty in operation in the dynamics of group psychology. Here Freud seeks to understand how groups form in modern societies, what libidinal bonds and energies tie members of the group together, and why individuals behave very differently in groups than when they are on their own, why they exhibit what social psychologist Gustave Le Bon called 'a thirst for obedience' (Freud, 1949: 21). At work is a kind of emotional contagion that emanates from the libido and leads to the abdication of one's own ego; a group of individuals, who otherwise have little in common, are bound together through the love instinct. For Freud, what makes this libidinous bond possible is the figure of the leader, who acts as a cipher of love and identification. As an example of an 'artificial' group formation – groups with leaders, as distinct from those without – Freud discusses the church, as a community of believers united around its leader, the symbolic figure of Christ, who is a kind of father surrogate. The Christian community is formed through the common bond of love – Christ's love for each of its members, and their love for him – a bond that also allows believers in the group to love one another as 'brothers in Christ'. The other example is the army, which is also based on the common principle of love and obedience to the commander. However, although both father figures – Christ and the commander – might seem relatively benign, they are still, as leaders of a group, exceptional sovereigns, who, because of their exceptionality, can demand of their followers absolute obedience and sacrifice – something also recognised by Schmitt in his understanding of the political group as a theologically based community of believers. Moreover, as Freud shows, in a further parallel with Schmitt's theory of political identification, the group is held together through a relation of enmity to those outside the group: even the church must be intolerant of unbelievers (ibid., 51).

So the leader, as the exceptional sovereign, becomes something like a love object that supplants the individual's own ego ideal. The follower loves his leader and believes he is loved *by* his leader; he puts his leader in place of his own ego ideal, which is why he often loses any sense of self-preservation and autonomy, and is even prepared to sacrifice himself for this object. There is a familiar Oedipal dynamic in evidence here – the love and identification of the child with his father. And it is no surprise, then, that behind the figure of the leader of the group there lies the old patriarchal figure of the primal father of the horde. The leader of the group, as a father substitute, is simply a sublimation of a much earlier and more traumatic figure, fear of whom is replaced, or at least combined, with love. This explains the exceptional power and authority of the leader as the one who constitutes the group by standing outside it and exempting himself from the rules that govern others, being the point of love and identification among his followers: 'Even to-day the members of a group stand in need of the illusion that they are equally and justly loved by their leader; but the leader himself need love no one else, he may be of a masterful nature, absolutely narcissistic, self-confident and independent' (ibid., 93).

It is not difficult to see here the shadow of the future fascist master, the totalitarian leader waiting in the wings, the dangerous potentiality haunting Freud's thinking. All societies, no matter how democratically organised, are susceptible to the seductions of the exceptional sovereign, the charismatic figure of the leader, upon whom the fantasies and desires of individuals are projected. We see glimpses of this in our own time, with populist demagogues, authoritarian figures, little fathers, who emerge through democratic procedures, who claim to be of the people and to speak directly for them, while narcissistically revelling in their love and adoration. Yet the conclusion to be drawn from Freud's account is that the leader is a thing made by his followers; that his power over them flows ultimately from their idealisation of him and their relinquishment of their own power over themselves – the age-old problem of voluntary servitude diagnosed by Étienne de La Boétie (1942 [1548]). In a strange way, the logic of the exception is both undermined and reinforced with this claim. There need be nothing exceptional about the leaders in terms of their personal qualities, as long as people are prepared to *believe* in the exceptional force of their personality. Freud's psychoanalytic account of groups as phantasms of the primeval horde thus reveals something essential about the psychic bonds that structure contemporary societies and, once again, points to the desire for transcendence and to the place of exceptional power, real or imagined, which is the central focus and predicate of political theology.

The Superego

To understand these psychosocial bonds underlying the problem of political theology, we must further examine the question of guilt; and it is here that I turn to Freud's famous text *Civilization and Its Discontents*. For Freud, guilt is essentially the price we pay for our entry into the social order and is the result of the repressive restrictions, particularly on our sexual instincts, that civilisation imposes upon us. Civilisation is based on a trade-off, a psychosocial contract whereby, in return for security and peace, we agree to renounce satisfaction of our instincts, which become inadmissible in civilisation. Yet this arrangement results in neurotic suffering and guilt, as symptoms of our inability to cope with the demands and sacrifices that civilisation imposes upon us. Perhaps its most unreasonable demand is the biblical commandment 'Love thy neighbour as thyself' – a commandment to which Freud responds with astonishment and incredulity. Not only was this an unnatural expectation, but it is more natural to hate and fear our neighbour as a stranger who might do us harm, or as someone towards whom we are more inclined to behave aggressively (Freud, 1961a: 61). Yet it is these inclinations that we must suppress or sublimate into love and altruism.

However, so destructive are these aggressive drives within us – what Freud refers to as the 'death instinct' – and so dangerous are they to the social bond, that civilisation performs its most cunning trick of turning them back against us. Freud's well-known argument here is that the individual's encounter with external laws and prohibitions, first through patriarchal authority within the family, then through interaction with social institutions, induces him to internalise his aggressive instincts, to turn them back upon himself and towards his own ego, so that he is more likely to chafe against himself than against those around him. Thus we have the invention of guilt, the 'bad conscience' upon which civilisation is built. Aggressive instincts, turned back upon the individual, take the form of the superego, the voice of moral conscience that constitutes an internalised agency of self-policing and moral censorship. In this figure of the superego, in which, as Freud observes, there is a strong element of aggression, we detect once again the presence of the primal father in all his obscene excess. Freud talks about the way in which the superego is excessively severe and punitive, punishing the saint more than the sinner and seemingly taking delight in the individual's suffering (ibid., 72). In other words, the superego is more than the rational and moral agency of the law; it is also a sadistic agency that enjoys tormenting the subject with excessive guilt. The superego – the remnant of the primal father – is a kind of obscene supplement to the moral law, transgressing it in its excessive and sadistic enjoyment, while also enforcing it.

Lacan and the Name of the Father

For Jacques Lacan, who sought a 'return to Freud' through structuralist linguistics,[3] the symbolic figure of the father was also central. However, the father should be thought of as a 'master signifier', which Lacan formulates as S1. Insofar as it stands outside the symbolic order, the master signifier serves to guarantee and determine the order of meaning, anchoring or fixing relations between signifiers, so that they can be differentiated. The 'name of the father', as distinct from the real, flesh-and-blood father, is the symbolic point of authority, a key signifier that stands outside the chain of signifiers – like the sovereign point of exception (Lacan, 1993: 96). It is what Lacan calls the 'quilting point', a stitch in the fabric of signifiers that fixes meaning, if only contingently. The master signifier refers to the symbolic role of the father, who enforces the 'law of castration', in other words whose symbolic presence prohibits or mediates between the subject and his access to the object of desire, the mother, thus creating the distance from *jouissance* ('enjoyment') that is the mark of the subject's entry into the symbolic order. And, according to Lacan, it is the 'foreclosure' (*Verwerfung*) or radical exclusion of the name of the father, as this primordial signifier, from the subject's symbolic order that causes the disintegration of meaning characteristic of psychosis.

The psychotic delusions and auditory hallucinations experienced by Judge Schreber, who is the subject of Lacan's study of psychosis as he was of Freud's, may be seen as an example of this opening of the abyss – what Lacan described as an excess of meaning that at the same time means nothing at all, as it 'cannot be tied to anything' (Lacan, 1993: 85). Central to Schreber's delusions and hallucinations is the belief that God wants to turn him into a woman so he can have sex with him. We can clearly perceive, in this figure of a sexually harassing and persecutory God, the old obscene figure of the primal father, who has replaced or filled the void left by the symbolic name of the father that was somehow missing in Schreber. As Lacan formulates it, *what is foreclosed from the symbolic order returns in the real*: the subject experiences 'an irruption in the real of something he has never known, a sudden emergence of a total strangeness' (ibid., 86). In other words, the psychotic subject's exclusion of the symbolic father as the law of castration means only the return of the persecuting phantasm of the primal father, who lurks behind, in all his obscene excess, the law of prohibition; in Schreber's case, this phantasm takes the form of a perverse God seeking sexual congress. It seems that in the unfortunate Schreber all the elements of a psychoanalytic model of political theology are present: God, exceptional sovereignty, and sexual *jouissance* in excess of the law.[4] Can we see in Schreber, who was also a man of the law, a sort of psychotic double of Schmitt: one who reveals, and indeed embodies, the perversity of the law, the genuine obscenity of the state of exception that, for Schmitt, was the highest and most sacred expression of the law's authority? While the state of exception might be the structural guarantee of the law, it risks opening up an anomic void in which the very meaning of the law disintegrates.

For Lacan, as for Freud before him, the God of religion is the expression of the structural need for a place of transcendence, a point of exception outside the order of symbolic law. God is a master signifier, a symbolic father substitute, operating as a point of authority that is both external and internal to the subject, becoming the figure of moral prohibition, the voice of the superego, and fulfilling a structural function of anchoring meaning and of covering up the void or radical contingency of the symbolic order. That is why, for Lacan, the true meaning of atheism is not simply to say that God is dead – as we shall soon see, this only *reaffirms* his presence as an agency of the unconscious – but to recognise that the 'other', the symbolic order, in which we seek meaning and identity, is itself radically incomplete and lacking, that there is no name of the father, no big other, as Lacan puts it, who guarantees meaning and identity and who believes for us. The insight to be taken from Lacan is that there is no real point of exception, that the place of transcendence symbolised by God and the father is imaginary, that the primal father, who is not subject to the law of castration, is simply a fantasy.

God Is Dead and Religion Triumphs

Escaping our enthralment with God is no easy undertaking, however. Lacan is even more pessimistic than Freud about the prospects of overcoming religion. Indeed, in a press conference in Rome in 1974, Lacan pronounced the 'triumph of religion' and expressed doubts that psychoanalysis could prevail over religious belief: 'It [religion] will triumph not only over psychoanalysis but over lots of other things too. We can't even begin to imagine how powerful religion is' (Lacan, 2013: 64). So far from advances in science displacing religion, as Freud predicted, they actually provide further impetus for religious belief – particularly in ameliorating the distressing and anxiety-provoking effects of new scientific discoveries. This is a phenomenon even more evident in our time. Religion is both a reaction to science and a way of giving meaning to what Lacan would call the expansion of the real that science opens up. There is more to the 'triumph of religion', however. Religion, particularly monotheistic religion, is the discourse that structures the subject in his alienation within the symbolic order – as we have seen, for instance, in the alienating command 'love thy neighbour' and in the institutionalisation of the law of castration and prohibition. The figure of God as father substitute structures the unconscious of the modern secular subject, subjecting it to the law of the master signifier. That is why, for Lacan, religion is so intractable; even (or rather especially) in secular modernity it continues to provide the ground or structure of symbolic authority, regardless of whether we consciously believe or not. Even the non-belief of atheists is still structured through religious belief; God remains central to atheists, serving as the predicate for their non-belief. Thus atheism in a way only confirms the power of religion. This does *not* mean that God is *not* dead, however. Yet it is precisely his death – the event that marks the secular age – that allows religious beliefs to permeate and structure the unconscious, just as the collapse of the theological world allows theological concepts to permeate and structure political institutions. Lacan formulates the paradox in the following way:

> we know that God is dead ... However, the next step is that God himself doesn't know that. And one may suppose that he will never know it because he has always been dead. This formula nevertheless leads us to something that we have to resolve here ... namely that *jouissance* still remains forbidden as it was before, before we knew that God was dead. (Lacan, 1997: 184)

But why does God's presence continue to be felt beyond his death; why does *jouissance* continue to be forbidden, even though we know that God is dead? Lacan's point here is that the death of God, so far from removing the guarantee of the law of prohibition, only makes this prohibition stronger

– as we saw with the primal father of Freud, whose presence is felt more strongly in death than in life. We encounter here the central paradox of psychoanalysis: the removal of one form of external authority – symbolised in the death of God – does not lead to the subject's freedom but, on the contrary, to an internalisation and intensification of this prohibition. The neurotic, who fantasises over the death of his father, imagining that this will liberate him from prohibition and leave him finally free to enjoy, finds himself, upon his father's death, overcome with even greater inhibitions, which come to the fore to take the place of the external figure of authority. In reversing the line from Dostoevsky's *The Brothers Karamazov* ('God is dead; now everything is permitted'), Lacan says, ominously: '"God is dead" ... "Nothing is permitted anymore"' (Lacan, 2007: 106).

This suggests that behind the internalisation of prohibition, once embodied in the external authority of God (or the father), there is actually a *demand* for the law, in other words a desire that desires *not* be satisfied. For what could be more anxiety inducing than the full satisfaction of desire; what could be more traumatic than the encounter with the lost object of desire, than full sexual *jouissance* with the mother? Desire therefore needs its own limit, its own lack, precisely so that it can go on desiring; for the fulfilment of desire is at the same time the death of desire. Could it be, then, that we imagine that external forms of authority act as a barrier to our desire simply so that we have a space of transgression, so that we can sustain the fantasy of flouting the law, so that we cover up this deeper internal limit to desire? For once law is removed, there is no more transgression, and we finally have to come to terms with the deadlock at the heart of our desire. Perhaps this is why we invent such elaborate rituals to delay gratification. There is a complex dialectic, then, between prohibition and transgression. Rather than law simply acting as a limit upon desire, prohibition actually stimulates and incites it, and it does this by holding out the promise of an impossible enjoyment on the other side of the law. In creating a barrier between the subject and enjoyment, the law sustains the illusion of an ultimate satisfaction – the lost object of enjoyment, what Lacan calls the Thing (*Das Ding*) (see Lacan, 1997: 43–70) – awaiting him on the other side of this limit. So, in saying 'no' to desire, the law actually invites its own transgression. In other words, the law of prohibition acts as a veil that shrouds the emptiness and impossibility of full enjoyment, thus eliciting desire. The Thing, the ultimate object of our desires, only exists insofar as there is a law to prohibit it. As Paul said in his Epistle to the Romans, '[f]or I would not have known covetousness unless the law had said, "You shall not covet"' (see Lacan, 2013: 18).

The Failure of Freedom

So the breakdown of traditional forms of moral and social authority does not inaugurate the reign of freedom but rather instantiates a new regime of prohibition. This is why, for Lacan, the libertine project – and here he has in mind someone like de Sade, for instance, in whom he finds the obverse of the Kantian moral law, now transformed into the law of enjoyment (see Lacan, 2006: 645–67) – has been a historical failure: 'The naturalist liberation of desire has failed historically. We do not find ourselves in the presence of a man less weighed down with laws and duties than before the great critical experience of so-called libertine thought' (Lacan 1997: 4).

Where does this leave the question of freedom today? Are we, in these more permissive times, weighed down with laws and duties in the way Lacan described? I do not think it too strong to say that today, in our liberal democracies, we no longer have any idea what freedom means. The breakdown of traditional patriarchal forms of authority results not in an experience of freedom, but in a strange new unfreedom, in which the sources of authority in society are less distinct but, for that very reason, more pervasive; in which, with the weakening of the symbolic authority of the law, one encounters in its place a proliferation of petty rules and microdisciplines that govern every aspect of life, something that Foucault wrote about in his analysis of the disciplinary society (see Foucault, 1991). We see this in everything, from increased restrictions on smoking in public places to ubiquitous surveillance, to rules governing sexual harassment in the workplace and to the political correctness (PC) policing of speech in public discourse, especially on university campuses. The latter is an interesting example of the way in which a certain kind of radicalism, once expressed in the rejection of conservative and patriarchal authority, becomes a new kind of joyless and morally pious authoritarianism, absolutely obsessed with identifying and rooting out ever more hidden forms of 'microaggression' and with creating 'safe spaces' that, so far from being spaces of freedom, are in fact highly regulated and controlled. That liberal societies have turned out to be highly *illiberal* should not surprise us.

One can also find evidence of this strange reversal in political discourse. Where once politicians and elected officials – no matter how corrupt or personally flawed – aspired to embody the dignity of office and were regarded as austere figures of moral authority, they are now subjects of ridicule and general disdain, and indeed are expected to embody their own degradation. In place of the symbolic father, we now have what might be seen as 'perverse fathers' – clownish and openly transgressive figures, whose popular appeal comes from their flouting of the rules and norms of political discourse and from their complete mockery of the dignity of office – as we see with Donald Trump and his earlier prototype, Silvio Berlusconi. We glimpse in these figures the semblance of the primal father, or the father who winks at us obscenely behind the law, inviting its transgression. And yet this diminution of the symbolic authority of the father does not in any sense mean a weakening of political power but, on the contrary, the emergence of a new and as yet unsymbolised order of power that, because we no longer know where we stand in relation to authority, is potentially much more terrifying.

What You Want Is Another Master!

We can also see how the paradoxical inversion of law and transgression, precipitated by the death of God, complicates the central narrative of revolutionary politics. What if it was the case that the idea of political and legal authority played a necessary phantasmatic role in structuring revolutionary desire; what if it was the case that the revolutionary drive actually *needed* law and authority – the repressive structure of the state – in order to sustain itself and have something to oppose and transgress? And what if this was so precisely to preserve the illusion that full freedom (the satisfaction of revolutionary desire) was attainable only if this structure of authority were removed? As a hypothesis, what I am suggesting here is that symbolic authority – the prohibitive figure of the father or, in political terms, the state – is necessary in order to sustain revolutionary desire and that it might even serve as a sort of cover or excuse, justifying a certain revolutionary pathos. In other words, might it not be the case that a certain figure of absolute and repressive political authority allows us to say, effectively that *we would be truly free, were it not for the state that stands in our way*? Is there not a sense in which revolutionaries – and here we can include the anarchists discussed in previous chapters – fantasise about the all-powerful state that denies their freedom, in the same way in which they fantasise about the freedom that awaits them once this institution is destroyed? And are revolutionaries today not trapped in a sort of cul-de-sac, confronted as they are with a situation in which traditional political structures have lost, or are losing, their symbolic authority and are in a process of decomposition? Does the decomposition of God or the father not lead at the same time to a complete paralysis of revolutionary desire?

More worrying still, does this not lead to a secret desire, at the heart of revolutionary politics, to invent new forms of authority, to fill the empty place of power once again? If, as Lacan believes, our unconscious is still structured by the master signifier even after the death of God, then we are still enthralled to a place of transcendence and sovereignty. Indeed, the fraught experience of revolutions in the past has only confirmed this. And this is certainly what Lacan foresaw when he said to his rebellious students in the aftermath of the May '68 uprising: 'the revolutionary aspiration has only a single possible outcome – of ending up as the master's discourse. This is what experience has proved. What you aspire to as revolutionaries is a master. You will get one' (Lacan, 2007: 207).

The political and ethical challenge of psychoanalysis is to avoid falling into the trap of the master – which, as we can see, is also the politico-theological trap. For Lacan, psychoanalysis is a way of helping us to accept our own lack, to accept the fact that the other, as the place of transcendence with which we identity and in which we seek meaning, is itself deficient, lacking and ungrounded; that there is no 'Other of the other', no 'name of the father'. This realisation means that we no longer seek to resacralise the empty place of power. In other words, we no longer look to new masters to fill this structural gap, because every attempt to do so will be inadequate and doomed to fail. It is in this sense that psychoanalysis might be understood as a genuinely atheistic strategy. If political theology is based on the fantasy of transcendence and exceptional sovereignty, there might be alternative ways of situating ourselves in relation to political structures, ways that allow us to break out of this enthralment to the master (see ibid., 176).

Not-All: God and Feminine *jouissance*

Another way of thinking about this is through the feminine logic of sexuation. In his Seminar XX, Lacan outlines male and female sexual difference, once again as signifiers, as formal structural positions between which, furthermore, there is no natural complementarity: *Il n'y a pas de rapport sexuel* ('There is no sexual relationship'). However, for our purposes, the important thing here is the different ways in which these positions are structured in relation to the master signifier or the phallic function, which establishes the law of castration. In terms of the male position, all men are submitted to the law of castration, which is established, as we have seen, through the exceptional logic of the master signifier. Paradoxically, for all men to be submitted to the law of castration, there must be one who stands outside this law and whose exceptionality guarantees and enforces it; to close the set, to make it complete, there must be a point of transcendence that goes beyond it. For Lacan (1999: 79–80), '[t]he whole here is thus based on the exception posited as the end-point [*terme*]'. In Freudian terms, of course, this is the primal father of the horde, the one who stands outside the law of prohibition that he enforces on everyone else. As we have begun to perceive, this exceptional position is a fantasy, but it is a necessary structural fantasy that allows the male position to be established.

Women are also inscribed under the master signifier, the law of castration, but in a different way: while 'all men' are entirely included in their set (apart from the fantasmatic exception that makes the whole function), women are included in the form of what Lacan (ibid., 80) calls 'not-all' or 'not whole'; there can be no complete or universal signification of women, no essence of 'woman'. There is some aspect of woman that cannot be signified, which is not entirely subjected to the law of castration. While there remains, for women, the master signifier, there is some aspect of them that is indifferent to it; unlike men, they are not enthralled in the same way to the place of transcendence, to the fantasy of the primal father. Perhaps one can put it in these terms: there is an aspect of women's subjectivity that is 'excepted from the exception' (see Reinhard, 2005: 60–1) and that therefore means they are included, but in a set that is structurally open, and as *singularities*, rather than as part of a universal generality. There is some parallel here with Stirner's paradoxical idea of the union of egoists – a kind of open set in which individuals are included, or include themselves, on the basis of their own uniqueness and singularity rather than on the basis of their being part of a general category.

Does this mean that the woman's position escapes, or can be seen as a counterpoint to, political theology? For Lacan, woman's *jouissance* goes beyond the phallus; it opens onto infinity. This position is best captured in the experience of female religious mystics – such as the thirteenth-century Hadewijch d'Anvers – who, in their encounter with God, experience, as Lacan puts it, a *jouissance* they know nothing about, which is beyond signification. Lacan's point is that in taking up the feminine position, in placing oneself on the side of the 'not-all' – something that men can also do – one opens up an experience of infinity or, in mystical terms, another face of God, one based on feminine *jouissance*. And, as Lacan says, 'as that is also where the father function is inscribed, insofar as castration is related to the father function, we see that that doesn't make two Gods [*deux Dieu*], but that it doesn't make just one either' (Lacan, 1999: 77).

On this God, who is neither one nor two – a God who is, rather, *not whole* – it is impossible to found any kind of political theology, least of all the monotheistic, sovereign, Schmittian kind. No doubt this is a very singular form of atheism that Lacan leaves us with. But perhaps the most radical kind of atheism is not to deny God, but rather to affirm a God who is at the same time radically incomplete, lacking, not-all. To avoid the pitfalls of political theology, whose force is by no means diminished by secularism, perhaps we need to go beyond *simply* denying the existence or God, just as we need to go beyond *simply* transgressing the law and defying political authority. Perhaps, instead, we need an encounter with infinity formed through incompleteness, an experience of transcendence that at the same time is limited, lacking and, I would say, profane. It is only by thinking the profane in this radical way that we can possibly arrive at an exception to the exception, in which sovereignty is impossible; or, put another way, a theology beyond any possible politicisation.

4

Auctoritas non veritas

On the Sovereign

The previous two chapters showed that our secular horizon is still profoundly theological and continues to be haunted by the figure of God and by religious categories of thought and experience that leave their mark on modernity. Secularism leaves intact the place of the sacred, of transcendent authority once occupied by God, and it is around this vacant place that the problem of political theology continues to circulate.

Perhaps the central question of political theology is that of sovereignty. As we have seen in Schmitt, political theology is predicated on sovereignty: the sovereign is a reflection of the absolute authority and transcendence of God. But what exactly is sovereignty, seeing that Schmitt takes pains to differentiate it from the state? Moreover, how did the modern concept of sovereignty emerge in political thought, and how was it shaped by religion? Most importantly, we need to ask not only why the concept of sovereignty is so central to political thought but why this figure remains so intractable, why it returns to the centre of the contemporary political experience. We may not quite know what sovereignty is today, and no doubt it has become more opaque and ambiguous in the age of globalisation. Yet, while sovereignty might

be more enigmatic, while it might take on ever more phantasmatic forms, it still very much structures the political
imagination.

   If sovereignty today is a question without a clearly defined
answer, it is important to discover what lies behind this question. This chapter will consider three different understandings of sovereignty and its development in modernity – those
of Hobbes, E. H. Kantorowicz and Walter Benjamin. Yet,
while these thinkers trace the politico-theological genesis
of the state, they do so in ways that, I argue, challenge and
even 'desacralise' the Schmittian conception of sovereignty. I
will also explore the paradoxical relationship between sovereignty and democracy. While they are in some ways opposed
concepts, they have nevertheless been articulated together
historically and find form and meaning in and through each
other – a mutual interdependence that is playing out in
the renewed popular demand for strong sovereignty that
characterises contemporary politics. Central here is the idea
of constituting power, in which the 'will of the people'
reaffirms sovereign authority as a site of transcendence. In
seeking alternatives to this idea of constituting power and its
politico-theological impulse, I turn to Benjamin's enigmatic
idea of 'divine violence'.

The Mortal God

Schmitt's theory of sovereignty is in many ways indebted
to Thomas Hobbes, whom he describes as a 'truly powerful and systematic thinker' (Schmitt, 2007: 65), one whose
fundamentally pessimistic outlook on human nature led
inexorably to the conclusion that only an absolutist sovereign, to whom we owe unconditional obedience, could
guarantee peace and security. Schmitt was especially fond
of invoking Hobbes's famous maxim, *auctoritas non veritas
facit legem* ['authority, not truth, makes the law'] as a way
of encapsulating the sovereign's exclusive right to decide
and determine law. There is a clear parallel here between
Hobbes's (1985: 313) insistence that the 'the Sovereign ...

is not Subject to Civill Lawes' and Schmitt's notion of the sovereign exception. Indeed, if we take as the definition of sovereignty – whether expressed in the form of a monarch, a single leader, or even a democratically elected legislative body – the absolute right to determine law, then Hobbes's thought remains fundamental to the concept. It is also, as I shall show, the decisive turning point in the development of political theology.

Hobbes's theory is a consecration of the modern state as it emerged in the seventeenth century. Absolute sovereign authority, embodied in a unified entity of the state that would be distinct from ecclesiastical institutions, was seen as the only effective way of putting an end to the confessional wars and religious conflicts that had torn Europe apart for over a century. For Hobbes, as we know, the only way to put a stop to civil war – to escape the natural condition of *bellum omnium contra omnes* ['the war of all against all'], a formulation that served as a curious model for civil war, which usually implies a war between two sides or groups rather than a conflict between individuals – was through mutual covenant, in which freedom was sacrificed for security. In our promising obedience to one person, who thereby becomes our sovereign, the state or leviathan is borne. Leviathan is a collective body, literally a body politic, composed – as is depicted on the famous frontispiece of Hobbes's great work of 1651 – of the tiny bodies of individuals whose will it both embodies and alienates. The sovereign represents the people, it 'beares their person' (ibid., 227), as Hobbes says, and, in doing so, forms them into a single, unified political entity.

Importantly, the political sovereign establishes supremacy over religious authority. As is depicted on the frontispiece, leviathan towers over and dwarfs the church. Furthermore, Hobbes lists, among the many powers of the sovereign, the sole right to be the judge of all 'Opinions and Doctrines', by which he mostly means religious doctrines. The sovereign must have the power to determine the very 'truth of doctrines', because, in Hobbes's reasoning, 'Doctrine repugnant to Peace, can no more be True, than Peace and Concord can be against the Laws of Nature' (ibid., 233). In other words, the prerogatives of security, as determined by the sovereign, trump the truth of revelation, and therefore the sovereign must have the right to decide on matters of scriptural interpretation and to prohibit the circulation of 'seditious doctrines'. Hobbes's thought is haunted by the constant threat to peace and security posed by religious sources of authority. The conflict between the spiritual and the civil, between church and state, is dangerous and cannot be tolerated: '*Canons* against *Lawes*; and a *Ghostly Authority* against the *Civill*; working on men's minds, with words and distinctions that of themselves signifie nothing, but bewray (by their obscurity) that there walketh (as some think invisibly) another Kingdome' (ibid., 370). There can only be one kingdom, one commonwealth and one sovereign, and this, for Hobbes, is the political sovereign.

Hobbes's political philosophy marks the emergence of the modern secular state out of the fractured and divided fabric of medieval societies, where – since the time of the investiture controversy in the eleventh and twelfth centuries – power had been shared and fought over by the church and the sovereign, and there was no clear locus of authority. The modern state now secularises itself, establishing the proper boundaries between the political and the religious. Religion is consigned largely to the realm of private belief and to the public rituals that sanctify political authority. The state separates itself from the church, establishes itself on new foundations – those of consent rather than divine ordination – and affirms its authority over the religious domain. However, it is precisely this process of secularisation, in which sovereignty consolidates its autonomy by dividing itself from religious authority and by subordinating it to its own power, that is the central move of political theology. In charting this dynamic, Hobbes reveals himself as a political theologian par excellence. The controversies over Hobbes's own religious allegiances – whether he was an atheist, an agnostic, a religious sceptic or a theist, whether he was, in his theological references, displaying sincere belief or merely paying lip service to the religious conventions of his day – have abounded since his own time.[1] More recent scholarship has made much of the references to eschatology and prophecy in Books 3 and 4 of *Leviathan*, which are seen as a reflection of Hobbes's religious faith and as constituting a theologically inspired vision of politics in which the earthly sovereign's reign is temporal and finite and would be superseded by the reign of Christ's kingdom on earth (e.g. Pocock, 1989: 148–200).

However, my own understanding of the political theology at work in Hobbes is rather different and remains unconcerned with the question of his personal religious convictions or lack thereof. Hobbes's notion of the sovereign state is, I would argue, profoundly secular, but its autonomy from, and dominance over, religion is achieved through the incorporation of religious authority – of divine power – into its structures and mechanisms. The sovereign state now comes to occupy the place of the sacred once held by religion. The Hobbesian leviathan absorbs the energy of religion and adopts the symbols of theological authority, in order to establish itself as an autonomous locus of power. Put simply, in supplanting religion with politics, in subordinating theological to political authority, Hobbes effectively invents a new religion of the state, one that adopts the trappings of the old religion, but now puts these to work in the service of leviathan. We can see this political theology clearly in the reference to the state or leviathan as a 'Mortall God' to whom we owe obedience and reverence (Hobbes, 1985: 227). This mortal God – a totally heretical formulation – is endowed with the authority of the 'Immortal God', and yet is a subject of human artifice. It is part god, part man, part automaton – a strange composite creature whose offices and institutions are like the nerves, joints and limbs of a gigantic anthropomorphic machine, and whose 'Artificiall Soul' is sovereignty (ibid., 81). Sovereignty breathes life into this monster and puts it into motion, like the Cartesian 'ghost in the machine'. The sovereign is endowed with godlike power and is a figure we should be in awe of. Moreover, Hobbes refers to the parties to the agreement, out of which leviathan is formed, as members of a 'Congregation', and to the contract itself as a 'Covenant', once again emphasising the sacred, quasi-religious, mystical union that engenders the sovereign state. Yet, importantly, Hobbes breaks the direct link between men and God, arguing that the only real covenant can be between men and their sovereign (ibid., 230). The political sovereign replaces God at the centre of the universe, and overawes all his subjects who, 'though they shine some more, some lesse, when they are out of his sight; yet in his presence, they shine no more than the Starres in presence of the Sun' (ibid., 238).

A further glance at the intriguing image on the title page of *Leviathan* reveals Hobbes's particular politico-theological understanding of sovereignty. The colossal body of leviathan, depicted as a princely yet monstrous figure, wields in one hand a sword, which symbolises civil authority as well as the sovereign right to violence, 'the power of life and death' as Foucault (1978: 136) put it; and in the other hand he wields a bishop's crosier, which symbolises religious office. Thus political and theological authority are united. But the fact that they are both wielded by the secular prince indicates that the latter is subordinated and assimilated into the former. In the lower half of the frontispiece, beneath the city over which leviathan looms, one sees a series of tableaux divided into two columns on either side of the banner carrying the title of the work. On the left side are symbolisations of secular political and military power – a castle, a crown, a cannon, the arms and banners of war, and the scene of a battle. On the right appear the symbols of ecclesiastical authority – a church, a bishop's mitre, the thunderbolt of excommunication, inscribed tridents, and an ecclesiastical court. Once again, the two forces – earthly and spiritual, civil and ecclesiastical – are united where they were once opposed; but they are united under the single authority of the sovereign state. We might also recall that 'Leviathan' was the name given to the great whale or sea monster who appears in the Book of Job in the Hebrew Bible, which Hobbes employs to convey the awesome and terrifying power of the sovereign state – an instance, once again, of the incorporation of religious images and signifiers into the symbolic order of political power.

Hobbes's work must therefore be understood as a political theology of the modern state. It marks the decisive moment in which sovereignty secularises itself through a process of dividing itself from, subordinating itself to, and incorporating into its own body the theological dimension that hitherto confronted it with an alternative universe and rivalled its own power.[2] Through the establishment of the unquestioned supremacy of civil over religious authority, the sovereign state depoliticises theology, containing and neutralising its political energy and effectively consigning it to the realm of private belief. But, as Hobbes shows, this can only be achieved through a certain *theologisation* of the political, whereby the sovereign state absorbs the force of religion, adopting its symbols, wrapping itself around its sacred dimension, and occupying its place of transcendence.

The Hook That Snares Leviathan

Despite the clear parallels between their accounts of sovereignty, there are also important differences between Hobbes and Schmitt, and, in many ways, Hobbes's political theology of the modern state disturbs the very foundations of Schmitt's theory. The individualist ontology that informs Hobbes's thought, his insistence on the absolute right of self-preservation, coupled with his legal positivism, are hard to reconcile with Schmitt's profoundly anti-liberal political theology, based as it is on the idea of a hyperpoliticised community forged through an intense relation of enmity to the outsider. Hobbes's commonwealth, based on the protection–obedience pact, is *depoliticised*; it presents a serene vision of a liberal society of self-interested individuals who are free to conduct their private and commercial affairs and to go about their business – are free even to refuse to sacrifice their lives for their sovereign[3] – as long as they do not threaten the peace and security upon which their freedom depends. Individualism, self-preservation and security form the conditions of Hobbes's secular commonwealth, and this is surely very different from, indeed antithetical to, the kind of community of faith that Schmitt has in mind, in which sacrifice rather than self-preservation is the highest good.[4]

Furthermore, while Schmitt initially seeks in Hobbes a basis for his exceptional and personalistic theory of sovereignty, we find instead the Hobbesian sovereign to be a kind of function – albeit an important one – of the state body for which he (or it, if the sovereign is 'an assembly of men') is responsible. The sovereign is like the bland visage of leviathan, resplendent in the trappings of authority, anointed with divine power but, at the end of the day, nothing more than another part of the automaton's body. He calmly dispenses justice, keeps the peace, promulgates and interprets law – but there is little of the dynamism, intensity and drama of decision that Schmitt's more romantic vision of sovereignty conveys. While the Hobbesian sovereign has the function of representation, which is essential to Schmitt's approach, he is more of an *institution* than a person; he has no autonomous personality and is virtually indistinguishable from the state whose interests he must serve. While, for Schmitt, the sovereign must transcend the state and be clearly differentiated from it, in the Hobbesian model the sovereign seems to be assimilated into state. Indeed, this is one of the points Schmitt himself makes in a later and more critical appraisal of Hobbes, in which he argues that Hobbes's political thought is part of the history of the mechanisation of the state – the transformation of the state into a gigantic administrative apparatus, which culminates in the neutralisation of the political and the drowning out of sovereignty in the modern era. The autonomous, personalistic element proper to sovereignty is essentially absorbed into the state; the sovereign 'soul' becomes a mere component of the gigantic machine (see Schmitt, 1996a: 34–5).

There are further significant divergences between Hobbes and Schmitt, particularly in relation to their political theology, which leads to quite different conclusions. Not only is Schmitt's political theology more intensely 'theological' than Hobbes's more secular approach, which has security and peace rather than politico-theological war as its ultimate aim; but, from Schmitt's point of view, Hobbes's attempt to contain religious conflict essentially by separating religion from politics results in the erosion of the authority of the state itself. According to Schmitt, in drawing a distinction between the interior private domain—where there was a certain freedom of religious belief to which the state remained largely indifferent—and the exterior domain of public religious doctrine that was regulated by the sovereign in order to avoid religious conflict and preserve public peace, Hobbes opened up a crack in the edifice of leviathan that 'contained the seed of death that destroyed the mighty leviathan from within and brought about the end of the mortal god' (ibid., 57). This crack in the theoretical justification of the sovereign state was exploited by 'liberal Jews' like Spinoza and, later, Moses Mendelssohn,[5] who turned the distinction between private freedom and public obedience into the basis for a universal principle of freedom of thought and expression, and thus into a liberal individualism that would come to limit the rights of the sovereign and, in doing so, pull down the whole edifice of leviathan. Rather than the emphasis being on maintaining the authority of the state, for which reason a certain degree of residual freedom of belief might be tolerated as long as it was kept private, the state must now serve the interests of individual freedom and would eventually give way to this principle. So, for Schmitt, Hobbes's prudence in attempting to consign religion to the private domain and to separate inner freedom from outward obedience unwittingly paved the way for the modern culture of liberal pluralism, in which the autonomy of sovereignty would be eclipsed and the state would come to be seen as an administrative machine at the service of individual interests.

We can see here the different paths taken by Hobbes and Schmitt in their politico-theological thinking. While Hobbes seeks to depoliticise theology by containing it within the mechanism of the state, Schmitt seeks to preserve a certain theological intensity at the heart of the political, as its vital source energy. This is why, for Schmitt, the danger of separating private belief from public obedience is the liberalisation of leviathan; religious belief should not be divided from public obedience, but must become its very source and life essence. Yet the unity of theology and politics that sustains Schmitt's version of sovereignty is precisely what is undone by Hobbes.

The Two Bodies of the King

I have understood Hobbes's theory of the sovereign state as a decisive turning point in the fraught relationship between theology and politics – the point at which the theological is fully incorporated into the state and thereby neutralised as a competing force. Yet this was the culmination of a much longer process, preceding Hobbes by several centuries, in which the state gradually secularised itself and established its autonomy from religion. As Ernst H. Kantorowicz shows in his celebrated study of medieval political theology, the theory of the 'king's two bodies', as formulated by the crown jurists of the Elizabethan court in England in the sixteenth century, borrowed heavily from earlier religious and theological metaphors, in an attempt to establish the notion of a secular political state as distinct from church authority. The idea that the king had two bodies – a natural body that would die and be subject to the infirmities of sickness and old age; and a corporate, political body that represented the authority of the state and would never age or become infirm, but would live eternally (Kantorowicz, 1997: 7) – was a legal fiction devised in order to get around the problem of monarchical succession and affirm the sempiternity of the state. The problem presented by the death of a monarch – who in his own person incarnated the corporate entity of the state – was to explain how the authority of the crown could be maintained in the interregnum before the coronation of his successor. This necessitated the invention of the idea of a second, corporate body of the king – based originally on the idea of the eternal body of Christ – which made it possible to claim that, while the actual king might have died, the 'King never dies' (ibid., 313).

Kantorowicz's genealogy charts a long process of secularisation of theological ideas and religious rituals through which authority was gradually transferred from the church to the state, and the emphasis shifted from a theocentric kingship to a 'man-centred' kingship. Like Hobbes in his political theology, Kantorowicz highlights a process by which the state's autonomy from, and eventual supremacy over, the church is established precisely by borrowing its symbols and metaphors and by adapting canon law to its own ends, thus incorporating within itself the divine authority that was once the proper domain of the church. The state secularises itself by developing a 'royal Christology'; it lays claim to the spiritual sphere by clothing itself with theological concepts, crowing itself with the religious regalia and rituals that the church once had a jealously guarded monopoly over. Thus the Christian idea of the *corpus mysticum* – the mystical body of Christ, as invoked by Aquinas – for instance, was transferred by jurists from the church to the state. The state came to be seen as a corporate body, a fictitious person or the body politic, with the king at its head. The idea of sovereignty began to be modelled on the two natures of Christ and generated a kind of God-man, a '"twinned person", "Man by nature and, through his consecration, god by grace"' (ibid., 141). Christ thus became, increasingly, a juridical abstraction used to consecrate the secular state.

These theological metaphors provided the basis for the construction of the legal doctrine of the two bodies of the king. Here we have a kind of composite body, formed of two conjoined yet different entities. The Tudor lawyer Plowden describes this strange being:

a Body natural and a Body politic together indivisible; and [that] these two Bodies are incorporated in one person and make one body and not divers, that is, the Body corporate in the Body natural, *et e contra* the Body natural in the Body corporate. (Quoted in Kantorowicz, 1997: 438)

Yet this is not an entirely symmetrical relationship: in conjoining the two bodies into the one, the corporate political body becomes the more dominant and significant element of the relationship and exercises its mystical power over the mortal, natural element. Kantorowicz explains: 'Not only is the body politic "more ample and large" than the body natural, but there dwell in the former certain truly mysterious forces which reduce, or even remove, the imperfections of the fragile human nature' (Kantorowicz, 1997: 9). This becomes a paradigm, I would argue, for the political theology of the modern state, and parallels the nature of the relationship between the political and the theological that we found in Hobbes. Not only is the doctrine of the king's two bodies formulated, as we have seen, at the nexus of politics and theology, through the state's appropriation of theological ideas and metaphors, but it also crystallises the nature of this relationship: just as the natural body is assimilated and subordinated to the more significant corporate, political body, so is the theological element assimilated and subordinated to the superior political sphere of the state. In the doctrine of the king's two bodies, constructed out of theological metaphors and ideas, the domination of the political over theological is cemented. And the 'mysterious forces' that dwell in the body politic, which sanctify and purify the natural body, are precisely the forces that the state has gained from theology and that are now turned against the church and work to neutralise and contain religion within the political domain.

We should read Kantorowicz's genealogy of sovereignty in the same way as Hobbes's political philosophy: as an attempt to secularise sovereignty, to make it 'worldly'. In this way, Kantorowicz's approach to sovereignty is, I would argue, far removed from Schmitt's.[6] In direct contrast to Schmitt, for whom sovereignty is always expressed in one figure, Kantorowicz shows it to be always divided into two. The *person* of the sovereign, so important to Schmitt, is made ambiguous and uncanny by this strange, composite figure, this conjoined body, the two bodies in one, which Kantorowicz identifies. The dignity the sovereign supposedly bears in his person, embodied in the heroism of the great decision, is shown to be based on the flimsiest of legal fictions, often developed to mask the most mundane and venal of interests – such as the need to resolve land disputes in which the king was embroiled, or to solve the awkward problem of dynastic succession. Indeed, the doctrine of the king's two bodies is regarded with some derision by Kantorowicz, who classes it as a form of a 'slightly foolish' mysticism that appears 'pathetic and pitiful' in the light of day (ibid., 3). The mystical aura of sovereignty is thus stripped away in this analysis.

Furthermore, what happens when the composite body of the sovereign – this carefully stitched together legal fiction – falls apart? What happens when the natural, physical body becomes detached from the corporate body that otherwise redeems and sanctifies it? Of course, the doctrine of the king's two bodies was designed to deal with the eventuality of the king's death – the mystical, corporate body, symbolised by the crown, quickly passed on to the successor. However, Kantorowicz's discussion of Shakespeare's King Richard II describes a process in which the living king is slowly stripped of his royal authority, and we are left with the undignified spectacle of the king's symbolically naked, enfeebled and mortal body, the body that withers and dies: 'Let us talk of graves, of worms and epitaphs', says King Richard, as he ruminates on the prospect of his loss of sovereign authority. As Kantorowicz (1997: 30) puts it: 'Gone also is the fiction of the royal prerogatives of any kind, and all that remains is the feeble human nature of the king.' The slow, undignified decline of sovereignty, the separation of the two bodies of the king, and the return of the spectre of the enfeebled flesh, the 'bare life' that is hidden behind the visage of authority, are something that disturbs and unsettles the Schmittian figure of the sovereign. Do we not see the same undignified spectacle today in some of our contemporary sovereigns? The 'human all too human' figure of Trump, for instance, who creates such a scandal for the dignity of the office he occupies, throws into sharp relief the gap between the body natural and the body political and exposes the very imposture that is sovereignty.

The Impotent Sovereign

The masquerade of sovereignty is further revealed by Walter Benjamin in his work *The Origin of German Tragic Drama* (*Ursprung des deutschen Trauerspiels*), written partly as a response to Schmitt's *Politische Theologie*. This is a study of the literary genre of German baroque drama of the sixteenth and seventeenth centuries – once again at this crucial turning point in the history of sovereignty and political theology. Indeed, Benjamin sees the figure of the sovereign, as presented in this dramatic genre, as central to the worldview of the baroque age: 'The sovereign is the representative of history. He holds the course of history in his hand like a sceptre' (Benjamin, 1998: 65). The baroque sovereign, however, inhabits a world in the aftermath of the collapse of theology, in which the struggle for power takes centre stage, seeking to occupy the place of transcendence left vacant by religion. Yet, as Benjamin shows, charting the same politico-theological dynamic that I have been discussing, the place of transcendence passes from theology to politics. The sovereign of the baroque age, as represented in these dramas, is showered in divine metaphors; he is compared, for instance, with the sun, as we saw also in Hobbes (see Benjamin, 1998: 67). However, as the baroque age is a world without eschatology – there is no longer the promise of redemption, of the coming of Christ's kingdom – it is also a world haunted by the ever present spectre of catastrophe, in a constant state of emergency. The sovereign must therefore be equipped with exceptional, dictatorial powers to avert the state of emergency. We are very close here, in other words, to the Schmittian model of the sovereign as the one who decides on the exception and who has emergency powers, precisely in order to protect the state against existential threats.

Yet can the baroque sovereign live up to the responsibilities of the authority invested in him? On the contrary, so far from being the decisive sovereign whom Schmitt has in mind, the baroque sovereign of these dramas is utterly *indecisive*: 'The prince, who is responsible for making the decision to proclaim the state of emergency, reveals, at the first opportunity, that he is almost incapable of making a decision' (Benjamin, 1998: 71). The sovereigns of the baroque era are depicted as lacking resolve: they are always changing their minds and are subject to wild and unstable emotions that cause them, in the words of Benjamin, to 'sway about like torn and flapping banners' (ibid.). So much for the heroic decisiveness that Schmitt sought in the sovereign; so much for the one who unilaterally decides and acts, and takes responsibility for his decision. We have here instead a rather comical and ridiculous figure, the very parody of sovereignty: an impotent tyrant who can neither reign nor govern, which is why he is always the target of plots and conspiracies and why his downfall and martyrdom are often the subject of these dramas. There is a gulf between the transcendent authority the sovereign is expected to occupy and his inability to live up to his symbolic mantle, reflecting the gap between the two bodies of the king. As Benjamin says: 'The enduring fascination of the downfall of the tyrant is rooted in the conflict between the impotence and depravity of his person, on the one hand, and, on the other, the extent to which the age was convinced of the sacrosanct power of his role' (ibid., 72). In Benjamin's hands, the sovereign is profaned and brought down to earth. He sits on his throne, adorned with the regalia of sovereignty, but is incapable of fulfilling his role and exercising any genuine authority. He is a profane creature in a profane world: 'However highly he is enthroned over subject and state, his status is confined to the world of creation; he is the lord of creatures, but he remains a creature' (ibid., 85). There is nothing godlike about this sovereign.

The Return of Sovereignty

In the discussion so far, I have attempted to map out an alternative political theology of sovereignty to the Schmittian version we are more familiar with. In following the path by which the state secularises itself in early modernity, it is possible to arrive at an understanding of sovereignty that is more profane, worldly and even, in the case of Benjamin, somewhat dysfunctional. I will have more to say about Benjamin and his assault on state sovereignty later in the chapter. But we are left with the question of what sovereignty actually means today. In an era of globalisation, in which transnational flows of capital have eroded the authority and identity of nation states, the concept of sovereignty has become even more ambiguous and fractured. Is sovereignty still located within the borders of nation states and exercised by national governments – as it had been for centuries – or is it now to be found in a more abstract form, in transnational finance or in global networks of information and communication? In a time when global tech giants, for instance, often have more influence than national governments,[7] or when a global banking system can threaten the stability of national economies, the question of who or what wields *auctoritas* is entirely unclear. There is a sense in which sovereignty today is everywhere and nowhere; it is chaotically dispersed, fragmented, shared and fought over by national governments, international bodies, transnational companies, media conglomerates, police and paramilitary forces, and terrorist organisations. Indeed, it may be that there is no longer much analytical value in talking about sovereignty and that the growing disorder and anarchy that characterises our world – like the catastrophic horizon that haunted the Benjamin's baroque world – is symptomatic of the absence of any coherent and effective form of authority.

Maybe today's sovereigns, whoever they might be and in whatever form they might appear, are no more capable of mastering the global state of emergency – which they often themselves engender – than the inept sovereigns of the *Trauerspiel* were.

Yet it would seem that the idea of sovereignty never really goes away and that it continues to structure our political experience and imagination. Sovereignty resurfaces as a kind of apparition that traces the form of its own absence, as a symptom of its own loss. As the reality of the nation state, as a clearly delineated locus of sovereign authority, grows dimmer, the fantasy of sovereignty grows stronger. There is a demand for the reassertion of the authority and protection of the nation state, particularly in a time of economic uncertainty and global instability. Nation states are hence obliged to make a spectacle of their sovereignty and power. Whether more tightly patrolling borders and building walls,[8] attempting to restrict flows of migration, introducing tougher 'law and order' measures, engaging in meaningless military interventions, or making empty gestures and threats of war – the state has to be seen to be doing *something*, as a compensation for its lack of ability to really do anything. Furthermore, the desire for sovereignty is also expressed in the return of religion – often in fundamentalist and violent forms. Religion provides a point of collective identification, a symbolic figure of authority for people to rally around. Today, whether it is the evangelical movement in the United States and around the world, with its conservative political agenda, or Hindu or Jewish nationalism, or fundamentalist Islam with its fantasies of the caliphate, we see a return of sovereignty directly in the form of theology, unmediated by the secular state. It is as if the theological and the political are no longer held together by the mechanism of the state and the political containment of religion, which was the great achievement of secular modernity, is no longer operative – which is why religious intensity now spills out beyond the defined boundaries of the state and intersects with politics and movements of all kinds, in a much more unmediated and unstable way.

My claim here is that sovereignty today, insofar as it still exists, is a kind of *identity politics*, perhaps the ultimate form of identity politics. It becomes a vehicle or imago for expressing what is imagined as a coherent collective identity – whether that is religious, cultural or national. Every movement that groups itself around some kind of shared essence or identity makes a claim to sovereignty – that is, to a single, representative point of authority that holds this identity together and allows political claims to be made on its basis. Central to sovereignty, according to Derrida, is the idea of *ipseity*, meaning selfhood or individual identity, and implying a certain autonomy and self-referentiality: *ipse* is 'the one-self that gives itself its own law, of autofinality, autotely, self-relation, as being in view of the self, beginning by the self with the end of self in view' (Derrida, 2005: 10–11). As such, it also implies a certain self-determination and sense of freedom. Without a notion of sovereignty it is hard to have any experience of freedom or sense of control over one's own life, and, in a world that increasingly appears to us as being at the mercy of anonymous forces beyond the capacity of mortals to control, the notion of sovereignty as a reassertion of control – control by the people – becomes particularly appealing. Sovereignty becomes both prosthesis and prophylactic, constituting an illusion of power and protection. It was striking, for instance, that the slogan of the successful pro-Brexit side of the 2016 EU referendum in the United Kingdom was 'Take Back Control', seen in terms of a reclaiming of national powers from the impersonal institutions of the European Union. The vague, barely understood idea of 'sovereignty' was invoked time and time again as sort of talismanic fetish, a form of infantile 'wish fulfilment' that served as the central structuring fantasy of this campaign; as was the similarly meaningless idea of 'Making America Great Again' that was the central motif of the Trump campaign in the United States. We are dealing here with a notion of sovereignty at its most ideological, phantasmatic, and, I would say, *theological*, but also, and for this very reason, at its most compelling, as it is invested with real libidinal power.

Sovereignty and Democracy

It is here that we must reflect on the relationship between sovereignty and democracy. In recent times we have seen the resurgence of what is perhaps somewhat lazily termed 'populist politics'. Central to populism is the figure of 'the people', which is always connected to the idea of sovereignty. As we know from both Hobbes and Schmitt, the representative person of the sovereign is the figure that allows the people, as a unified political body, to be constituted. Of course, the signifiers of 'sovereign' and 'people' operate quite differently in left- as opposed to right-wing populist discourses, despite their potential, and sometimes actual, ideological promiscuity. While the populism of the left seeks sovereignty in the form of greater democratic control of the economy by the people and in a more egalitarian distribution of wealth and resources, the populism of the right seeks a direct identification between the people, as a national or cultural homogeneity, and the sovereign; and it is mobilised against the figure of the enemy or outsider, who is seen to threaten or dilute this identity – typically, today, the immigrant or the Muslim. Moreover, it is striking the degree to which the populism of the right pitches itself as a kind of democratic revolt of ordinary people against 'elites', who represent the forces of liberalism and globalism. The populism of the right today is a kind of conservative 'revolution' that seeks to reconstitute a more direct and more genuine idea of sovereignty. It sees itself as wresting sovereignty back from the control of elites who have sacrificed it on the altar of globalism, who have watered it down and reduced it to technocratic governance. It is also a deeply nihilistic rejection of any sense of international ethical or legal responsibility, particularly when it comes to commitments to human rights or the environment; the isolationist doctrine of 'America First', with its racist undertones, projects the fantasy of the nation state with closed borders, detached from any moral responsibility to the burning world outside, believing in nothing other than its own identity and valuing nothing other than its own enjoyment.

Of course, the popular revolt against 'the establishment' always generates a new kind of establishment, which inevitably ends up alienating the 'will of the people' just as much as the establishment it replaced; such is the fate of every populism. At the heart of populism is the desire for the figure of the leader-sovereign, the one who holds the people in his loving or authoritarian embrace, who maintains the illusion of protection against the uncertainties of the outside world and exercises over the people the kind of hypnotic power of suggestion that Freud noticed in the dynamics of group psychology. Democratic systems around the world at the moment seem to be throwing up 'strong man' leader types, those who try – in almost a self-parodying fashion – to incarnate the place of sovereignty, whether in the form of the machine-gun toting Duterte in the Philippines, the self-styled 'illiberal democrat' Orban in Hungary, the bare chested Putin of Russia, the meglomanical 'sultan' Erdogan in Turkey, or the erratic and brittle Trump. These slightly comical and absurd figures, crude caricatures of power, perform a theatre of sovereignty, each displaying, in his body, speech and mannerisms, in his outrageous utterances and unpredictable behaviour, different faces of sovereignty, whether violent and phallic or puerile and narcissistic. All of these little sovereigns try to convey a certain transgression or violation of the norms and codes of the office they hold or of the constitutional system they are supposed to maintain, staging a confrontation between the people and the political order. They are figures of what might be called the democratic exception – they emerge through the democratic system but, when in power, often introduce measures that quite seriously threaten democratic mechanisms such as media freedom and judicial independence. They are somehow both inside and outside the constitutional system, embodying, or attempting to embody, the place of the exception, yet with none of the dignity and gravitas that Schmitt associated with the sovereign decision. More so, they take to heart – albeit, once again, in an exaggerated and parodying way – Hobbes's maxim *auctoritas non veritas*. The current paradigm of 'post-truth' politics – a cliché,[9] but no less real for all that – of which these leaders are both symptoms and master manipulators, suggests that truth in politics, such as it was, has now lost any sort of symbolic value and is entirely a plaything of power.

We have to remind ourselves that these now normalised violations of constitutional and discursive norms take place within democracies and are apparently endorsed by large sections of the voting public. The populist sovereign, like the classical figure of the demagogue – regarded by the philosophers as poisonous to the polity – manages to turn democracy against itself; he mobilises the democratic will of the people against democracy, and in the name of taking a wrecking ball to the 'establishment' ends up destroying democracy itself. We are witnessing something like what Derrida terms the suicidal or 'auto-immunising' impulse of democracy (see Derrida in Borradori, 2003: 85–136), whereby democratic systems, in their openness and instability, end up destroying themselves by either securitising themselves to death or (as we see at the moment) electing to power authoritarian political forces that threaten to restrict democratic rights and freedoms. It is unclear whether this authoritarian populist turn in democracies is the last gasp of a political system that is now exhausted, or whether democracy can redeem itself in more genuine and less dangerous ways in the future – avoiding both populism and the technocratic politics of neoliberalism that produces it. But the recent experience of democracy should remind us that there is nothing intrinsically redemptive about democracy itself and that there is always the danger of the demos becoming tyrannical. The old problem of the 'tyranny of the majority' has lost none of its relevance today, as we observe the way in which the mystical and sacred notion of the 'will of the people' is invoked as absolute and unquestionable. Sovereignty is now expressed in the form of a demotic power that brooks no dissent; the 'will of the people' is ominously suspended above our heads as a permanent threat. As we now see in the aftermath of the EU referendum in the United Kingdom, the will of the people must be obeyed at any cost.

Democracy is not, therefore, necessarily opposed to authoritarianism, and its procedures are by no means an adequate safeguard against it. Schmitt himself proposed a model of authoritarian democracy based on plebiscite and acclamation – a technique, we should recall, also employed by the fascists in Italy in the 1920s and 1930s. Schmitt sought to distinguish between liberal parliamentary institutions and the democratic will of the people – which he saw in terms of a strong identity between the ruler and the ruled:

> Compared to a democracy that is direct, not only in the technical sense but also in a vital sense, parliament appears an artificial machinery, produced by liberal reasoning, while dictatorial and Caesaristic methods not only can produce the acclamation of the people but can also be a direct expression of democratic substance and power. (Schmitt, 2000: 16–17)

There was therefore no incompatibility between democracy and dictatorship – on the contrary, dictatorship offered a much closer relationship between the people and their leader. Obviously this is a highly singular and narrow conception of democracy that Schmitt presents here, one that takes no account of constitutional mechanisms and ideas of individual rights, which, while they emerge from a liberal rather than strictly democratic tradition, have nevertheless been historically incorporated into a broader understanding of modern democracy. However, in seeing sovereignty – and, for Schmitt, this can only ever be an authoritarian concept – as central to democracy, he touches on what is essential to it: democratic decision making can only be articulated in terms of a single will, and can thus only be expressed in terms of sovereignty. There is, then, a rather paradoxical relationship between democracy and sovereignty: while democracy implied, for ancient philosophers like Plato and Aristotle, a kind of unstable, anarchic rule of the many – the demos – it is always attached to '-cracy' as a form of rule, power and sovereignty, which, by definition, is singular. So democracy is wrapped around sovereignty; democratic decisions must be articulated through some kind of sovereignty. Democracy is therefore dependent upon a *force* that at the same time contradicts and threatens it (see Derrida, 2005: 13).

Moreover, for Schmitt, at the heart of every constitutional order is the sovereign, 'constitution-making' will of the people from which it emerges. This will, which is unmediated, is to be distinguished from the constitutional norms that it establishes: 'A constitution is not based on a norm, whose justness would be the foundation of its validity. It is based on a political decision concerning the type and form of its own being, which stems from its political *being*' (Schmitt, 2008: 125). 'Constitution-making' power has a theological dimension – it was, in Schmitt's analysis, originally seen as the constituting power of God (his power to create the universe) – before it was passed, through the hands of absolutist monarchs, to the people, in the notion of *pouvoir constituant* as formulated by Abbe Sieyès at the time of the French Revolution.

Sovereign and Divine Violence

This nexus between 'constitution-making', or *constituting*, power and *constituted*, or state, power is the subject of Benjamin's famous essay of 1921, 'Critique of Violence' ('Zur Kritik der Gewalt': Benjamin, 1986a). We should read Benjamin as an important interlocutor and critic of Schmitt, particularly in relation to his understanding of sovereignty. The subterranean dialogue between Schmitt and Benjamin, like that with Taubes, not only reveals important aspects of Schmitt's thinking but also illuminates alternative pathways through the politico-theological problematic. Not only was Benjamin's discussion of the baroque a response to Schmitt's theory or sovereignty, but it is also possible to see Schmitt's 1922 work on political theology as itself a response to Benjamin's essay on violence from the previous year.[10] Schmitt's sovereign state of exception, as a kind of counterrevolution designed to neutralise the threat of anarchism, might be interpreted as a response to Benjamin's notion of 'divine violence', which is influenced by a certain understanding of anarchism and which invokes a 'real state of exception'[11] where state authority is radically deposed.

Paradoxically, revolutions and counterrevolutions often share the same structure – both gravitate around sovereignty and both affirm its place of transcendence and authority. While the counterrevolution safeguards the constitutional state order by suspending it in the state of exception – thus creating, artificially, a situation that resembles a revolution – a revolution destroys an existing constitutional state order only to erect a new one in its place. The core of sovereignty and power is retained in both. As we have seen in Schmitt, the 'constituting will' of the people, as exercised in the French Revolution, was a form of sovereignty and erected, in the place of the old system, a new constitutional regime, a new order of sovereign power and authority. What was important and valuable about the French Revolution, according to Schmitt, was that it retained throughout a notion of *political unity*, embodied in the people, as the true locus of sovereignty – which is why it could create a new political order on the ruins of the old. Indeed, the concept of state sovereignty was preserved in this political unity, which is why there was no problem of the discontinuity of the French state (Schmitt, 2008: 141–2). We might say that this notion of political unity is the modern form of the king's mystical, corporate body politic. In revolutions, sovereignty is preserved in the form of its constituting power, and even intensified in the interregnum between the old regime and the new. So, revolutions, at least in their classical form, reinvent the place of authority they overthrow; they are still caught up in the politico-theological trap. The challenge taken on by Benjamin in his essay on violence, then, is to escape this continual oscillation between constituting and constituted power, between the counterrevolution that preserves the existing order and the revolution that destroys the existing order only to found a new one in its place.

In developing an ethical critique of violence that is not reliant on law, Benjamin draws a distinction between two forms legal violence – 'lawmaking' (*rechtsetzend*) violence and 'law-preserving' (*rechtserhaltend*) violence. Lawmaking violence is a form of violence – like revolutionary violence or military conquest – that founds a new legal order, and may thus be likened to *constituting* power. Law-preserving violence preserves the existing order, and thus can be seen as *constituted* power. The point is, however, that these two forms of violence ultimately blur into each other. The main example Benjamin gives here is that of the police, in whom these two registers of violence are combined 'in a kind of spectral mixture' (Benjamin, 1986a: 286). The violence of the police is law-preserving, in the sense that it enforces existing laws; but it is also lawmaking because, in enforcing these laws, the police often exceed their limits and, in doing so, expand the boundaries of legal authority, arbitrarily intervening and deciding 'where no clear legal situation exists' (ibid., 287). The police, then, are a literal embodiment of the sovereign state of exception, yet one that is not 'exceptional' at all, but everyday and mundane: it is 'formless, like its nowhere-tangible, all-pervasive, ghostly presence in the life of civilized states' (ibid.). The arbitrary power and violence routinely exercised by the police around the world, including in liberal democracies supposedly based on the rule of law, is often striking to the eye; these petty sovereigns, who at times seem indistinguishable from paramilitary forces or private armies, appear to constitute an almost autonomous form of power in society, which at times seems to be beyond the direct control of the constitutional order.

To escape this interminable dialectic between law, power and violence that constitutes the mysterious core of sovereignty – its force or authority[12] – Benjamin proposes an altogether different order of violence. 'Divine violence' is a form of violence that is no longer bound to the law, in either preserving or destroying the constitutional order. In this sense, it is different from, and opposed to, the 'mythic' dimension of sovereign violence that generates legal authority and fixates the subject, through guilt, to the order of the law and power.[13] Mythic violence is on the side of power, while divine violence is on the side of *justice*. Divine violence breaks the link that binds together violence and law and, in doing so, embodies the radical dissolution and transcendence of state power: 'On the breaking of this cycle maintained by mythic forms of law, on the suspension of law with all the forces on which it depends, finally therefore on the abolition of state power, a new historical epoch is founded' (Benjamin, 1986a: 300). How should we understand that this enigmatic notion of divine violence, which strikes without warning, is lethal without spilling blood and manages to disrupt the entire order of sovereign power, yet is not 'revolutionary' in the law-constituting sense? There is a clear anarchistic dimension to Benjamin's thinking here; and, indeed, the notion of divine violence might be seen as a sort of 'theological' – or, more exactly, messianic – interpretation of the French anarcho-syndicalist Georges Sorel's notion of the 'proletarian general strike', which is invoked directly in Benjamin's text. This is a form of action symbolically based on warfare – on the 'myth' of class war – but is not in itself physically violent and seeks to avoid rather than capture the structures of state power, through the autonomous self-organisation of the proletariat (see Sorel, 2004). We thus have here a model of radical action that avoids the twin poles of constituting and constituted power and violence; it seeks neither to preserve the existing state order nor to overthrow and reconstitute it. Rather it attempts to bypass state sovereignty altogether by organising life and social relations outside its control, thus bringing about a much more radical and 'violent' dissolution of the authority of the sovereign. Divine violence, which I suggest is modelled on this notion of the proletarian general strike, is, for Benjamin, violence as *pure means*, without any predefined end.

In embodying the possibility of living beyond state sovereignty, of freeing the subject from his enthralment to law, divine violence is a sort of messianic promise of the redemption of life. Benjamin defines it as 'a retribution that "expiates" the guilt of mere life – and doubtless also purifies the guilty, not of guilt, however, but of law. For with mere life the rule of law over the living ceases' (Benjamin, 1986a: 297). In this sense, it offers the possibility of a 'real' state of exception, as opposed to the 'false' state of exception that Schmitt gives us, in which the actions of the sovereign are still, in a way, bound to the law that it suspends, and that still works for the preservation of the legal order even as it violates it. Divine violence, by contrast, severs this link between sovereignty and law, which is why Benjamin says, finally, that divine violence, as 'sign and seal but never the means of sacred execution, may be called sovereign violence' (ibid., 300).

So we end up here with an idea of sovereignty and sovereign violence that is completely severed from the paradigm of the law. We need to think about what this could mean. Benjamin understands this in messianic terms, as the promise of liberation from the order of state power. In this sense, it is similar to the revolutionary eschatological dimension that Taubes finds in Paul. Yet Benjamin's messianism is *this*-worldly and profane. It is not the divine kingdom that awaits us at the end of history, but rather the order of the profane as the order of happiness (Benjamin, 1986b). It is difficult to translate this directly into either theological or political terms, which is perhaps precisely the point. While it is no doubt an incredibly, and perhaps hopelessly, enigmatic concept, I have sought to understand *divine violence* in terms of a certain ethics and politics of anarchism. Yet this is also a different kind of anarchism from the firebrand revolutionary variety we are familiar with from Bakunin; it is perhaps closer to what I will call a 'spiritual anarchism' – a concept I will elaborate in a later chapter.

5

Pastoral Power and Political Spirituality

Foucault and Political Theology

In this chapter I wish to discuss another thinker who seeks to desacralise the sacred dimension of power and authority, not so much through a messianic eschatology – as we saw previously with Benjamin – but through a patient genealogical analysis of the institutions and practices that govern us. Although Michel Foucault never refers explicitly to the problematic of political theology, his genealogical analyses of the mechanisms of power in secular modernity reveal their religious origins, the way they emerge out of ecclesiastical institutions and practices. However, I will suggest that Foucault's contribution to political theology in a sense turns this paradigm on its head and signals a radical departure from the Schmittian model. Foucault does not seek to sanctify power and authority in modernity, but rather to disrupt their functioning and consistency by identifying their hidden origins, unmasking their contingency and indeterminacy, and bringing before our gaze historical alternatives. Furthermore, Foucault introduces into the debate around political theology something that was entirely missing from it: the idea of the subject. The notion of the 'confessing subject' – the individual who, from earliest Christian times, has been taught to confess his secrets and thus to form a truth about himself – is central to Foucault's concerns, as are the ethical strategies through which the subject might constitute himself in alternative ways that allow a greater degree of autonomy. And while, in the past, religious institutions and practices – particularly the Christian pastorate – have sought to render the subject obedient and governable, at other times, including in modernity, religious ideas have been a source of disobedience, revolt and what Foucault calls 'counterconducts'. It is here that I will develop the idea of 'political spirituality', showing how this notion can operate as a radical counterpoint to political theology.

'We Need to Cut Off the King's Head'

If we are to find in Foucault a form of politico-theological analysis, it could not be more different from Schmitt's. Where Schmitt develops a 'sociology' of juridical and political concepts derived from theology in order to understand modern sovereignty, Foucault's genealogical analysis of power seeks to deliberately decentre the sovereign paradigm based on law. In an interview in 1977, Foucault said, famously: 'What we need, however, is a political philosophy that isn't erected around the problem of sovereignty or, therefore, around problems of law and prohibition. We need to cut off the king's head. In political theory that has still to be done' (Foucault, 2002a: 122).

The operation of power in modernity had shifted from a paradigm based on the juridical power of the sovereign – symbolised by his right to take life – to one of disciplinary biopower, which functioned from multiple sites and institutions in society, aimed at the control, administration and surveillance of individual bodies and populations, and was not primarily repressive or violent but sought, as Foucault put it, to 'make life live'. This did not mean, according to Foucault, that the question of sovereignty disappeared with modernity; indeed, in many ways this problem had become more acute, as his example of Nazi biopolitics and its reassertion of the old sovereign prerogative of killing showed (see

Foucault, 2003). Rather it meant that the juridical authority of the sovereign – the sovereign's absolute right to determine law – was no longer the fundamental model through which relations of power were organised. The law itself starts to function more as a mechanism of normalisation and regulation, in collaboration with a variety of other medical and administrative apparatuses. Governments still make and enforce laws, of course – in fact more laws than ever – but law no longer really has the function of symbolising the sacred authority of the sovereign or of displaying its 'murderous splendour' (Foucault, 1978: 141). The sovereign's absolute right to determine and, ultimately, suspend law through the state of exception, which was of utmost significance for Schmitt, was, for Foucault, no longer really central to modernity. Nor was the sovereign function of unifying the political field through the designation of the enemy: power, according to Foucault, 'does not have to draw the line that separates the enemies of the sovereign from his obedient subjects'; rather 'it effects distributions around the norm' (ibid., 144).

That Schmitt takes the juridical concept of sovereignty to be central to political analysis would indicate that, on Foucault's reading, he remains trapped within a paradigm that is now outdated: that there is something anachronistic (perhaps deliberately so) about Schmitt's attempt to bestow on the modern sovereign a certain sacred, theological dimension by comparing his authority with God's. This idea of sovereignty would be, from Foucault's perspective, part of a 'juridico-political' fiction, a hangover from premodern monarchical societies; and behind this quasi-theological image of sovereignty there is concealed a whole panoply of disciplinary and biopolitical techniques and strategies that this model simply cannot account for.

The differences between Foucault and Schmitt centre, I would suggest, around the question of the utility and value of political theology. If one takes political theology, as Schmitt does, as a way of understanding, and indeed affirming, the transcendent dimension of state sovereignty in modernity, then this is something Foucault would reject.

Indeed, one of his key methodological aims is to 'demytholo-gise' the state, to strip it of its metaphysical abstractions, and to understand it not as a single unified entity with a sover-eign soul, but as a heterogeneous and historically contingent set of processes and practices. In response to a certain fet-ishisation of the state – and here we might think not only of Schmitt and his sacralisation of the sovereign dimension of the state but also of anarchists and their radical opposition to the state as the source of all domination – Foucault (2007: 109) says: 'After all, maybe the state is only a composite reality and a mythicised abstraction whose importance is much less than we think.' Foucault's key methodological concern here is, as I would put it, to *detheologise* power, to desacralise it or strip away its sacred dimension. Rather than power determining a transcendent place in society, which in a way constitutes the illusion of its own omnipotence, it is maybe more productive to see it as a series of practices that are not theologically sanctified but historically determined, and therefore are contingent and reversible. Foucault says that the aim of his analysis is not to develop a general theory of power – which would turn power into an abstraction, Power with a capital P – but rather 'to put a stop to repeated invocations of the master as well as to the monotonous asser-tion of power. Neither power nor master, neither Power nor master, and neither one nor the other as God' (ibid., 56). Power exists, and is 'everywhere'; but it has no single identity or transcendent authority – no sovereign soul. It is nothing more than a historically contingent series of practices, alter-natives to which are always possible. If this is not a rejection of political theology *tout court*, then it is certainly a rejection of the kind of political theology that fetishises power and works in the service of the sovereign state.

Pastoral Power

Foucault's analyses of modern practices of power, however, also reveal their roots in religion, and are thus aimed at exposing the theological origins of supposedly secular institutions – and in this sense, they contribute to a broader, non-state-centric understanding of political theology. In his 1977–8 lecture series *Security, Territory, Population*, Foucault conducts a genealogical analysis of practices of security and government that started to emerge in the sixteenth and seventeenth centuries. In charting the transition from a premodern, sovereign-centric and theologically based paradigm of power to the modern paradigm of what Foucault calls government, he shows how the problem of the politics was no longer the safety of the prince and the preservation of his territory, but rather the security of the population. In this sense, the problematic of government starts to overlay and supplant the idea of sovereignty. It introduces a sort of division into the function of sovereignty: the sovereign must not only reign, he also, and more importantly, must govern, and governing implies a very different set of practices and techniques, which are concerned with the management of populations and the preservation of the state. The new 'art of government', what Foucault calls *politiques* – which he compares to a religious heresy because of its fundamental break with old 'cosmo-theology' that once defined the function of sovereignty – was thus concerned with the problem of *raison d'état* (Foucault, 2007: 345–6). This new imperative of governing, to which the sovereign was henceforth subjected and in the name of which his rights would be limited and he could even be overthrown, reminds us of the baroque sovereign who features in Benjamin's discussion of *Trauerspiel*. The important point here is that, while the emergency powers of the sovereign are extended,[1] his juridical person is diminished. Sovereign authority submits to a new rationality of government, which has its own priorities and objectives beyond those of the law, and which will ultimately be the judge of the efficacy of the sovereign. Put simply, governmentality achieves precisely what Schmitt abhors in modernity – the neutralisation of the transcendental dimension of sovereignty and its absorption into the administrative functionality of the state.

As Foucault's genealogical analysis shows, this new practice and idea of governing, as opposed to ruling, has its origins in the Christian pastorate and in the notion of pastoral power. Central to the pastorate is the shepherd–flock relationship, a motif that originated in the pre-Christian east, in the Hebrew idea of God as the shepherd of his people, but that became incorporated into the church and monastic institutions in the West during the early Christian period. Just as the shepherd leads his sheep to new pastures, the pastor guides his flock to their salvation. Pastoral power is the power of care and individualisation: the welfare of each sheep, each individual follower, is important to the pastorate, indeed, as important as the entire flock. As Foucault says, 'the shepherd must keep an eye on all and each, *omnes et singulatim*' (ibid., 2007: 128). Thus the paradox of the pastorate is that not only must the pastor or shepherd be prepared to sacrifice himself for his flock, but he must be prepared to sacrifice his entire flock for one of its individual members. This amazing logic of duty and self-sacrifice is very different from the sovereign paradigm, based on conquest and self-glorification.

Central to the relationship of pastoral power, which, according to Foucault, remains distinct from and runs alongside political power, is the relationship of obedience. The pastor who governs his flock is not a sovereign, nor does he exercise juridical power, but he nevertheless insists on obedience from its members. There is a relationship of complete submission – which we see typified in monastic institutions – of one individual, not to the law, but to another individual who guides him (ibid., 175). An individual obeys not in order to achieve some particular end, but purely for the sake of obedience itself; and the one who commands does so not for any egoistic reasons, but out of duty to God. For Foucault, what is important here are the forms of subjectivation involved: the subject of the pastoral relationship is not only one who submits, but one who forms a truth about himself through an examination of his conscience under the spiritual guidance of another, a process that binds him all the more tightly to the pastor. Foucault describes this as 'a mode of individualization by subjection [*assujettissment*]' (ibid., 184). Pastoral power involves the conduct or direction of another's behaviour – first in the form of spiritual guidance and confessional practices, and later in the form of general strategies of government. Indeed, Foucault takes this notion of conduct, of *conducting* – not so much forcing or coercing – the behaviour of another, as his general definition of relations of power: 'The exercise of power is a "conduct of conducts" and a management of possibilities' (Foucault, 2002c: 341).

Foucault is concerned, therefore, with the relationship between the Christian pastorate and ideas and practices of government that started to emerge at the end of the theological era. It is not so much that the pastoral functions of the church were mapped directly onto the state, but rather that during the sixteenth century there was what Foucault describes as an intensification of the religious pastorate, not only in its spiritual forms, but in an expansion of its temporal power and its concern with matters of everyday life, such as property and the education of children. At the same time, there was the growing concern with the conduct and government of lives beyond ecclesiastical institutions (Foucault, 2007: 229–31). This is a process Foucault describes as the 'governmentalisation' of the state, whereby, in parallel to religious conduction by the church, there arose new forms of 'public conduction'. And it was at the intersection between these two domains of conduction that the modern understanding of government started to develop. Foucault's politico-theological analysis – if indeed we can call it that – therefore approaches the question of secular politics and its relation to religion in terms of the interplay not so much between church and state, but between the pastorate and government:

> In other words, in modern Europe at least, the fundamental problem is undoubtedly not the Pope and the Emperor, but rather the mixed figure, or the two figures who ... share

one and the same name of minister. The minister, with all the ambiguity of this word, is perhaps the real problem and where the relationship between religion and politics, between the pastorate and government, is really situated. (Ibid., 191–2)

It is difficult perhaps to grasp today the function of this uncanny figure of the minister, whose polysemic significance we must nevertheless remain attentive to. The minister is clearly different from the sovereign, presenting a rather less dignified and august figure, one whose role is technocratic administration or governing rather than ruling. Yet, if ministers are our secular priests today, they appear to offer very little in the form of either care or salvation, operating rather as symbolic nodes of authority within a governmental apparatus that they no longer really control and that, in any case, seems no longer entirely operative and can no longer minister to the needs of society.

The Confessing Subject

Fundamental to Foucault's understanding of both modern power and modern subjectivity is the practice of confession. Indeed, as Foucault shows, the confession, which once again goes back to early forms of Christianity and becomes progressively institutionalised and 'secularised', finding its way, in the modern era, into all sorts of institutional apparatuses such as medicine and psychiatry, is precisely what attaches the subject to certain norms and discourses, to a certain 'truth' and identity that have been produced for him and that render him governable. 'Western man', Foucault says, 'has become a confessing animal' (Foucault, 1978: 59). Ours is a decidedly confessional society and culture, where rituals of confession are everywhere – not only, or even primarily, in religious contexts, where we once confessed our sins, but also in psychiatric and medical settings, in which the patient 'confesses' his maladies to the specialist who plays the role of the priest, interpreting symptoms and bringing to light the truth of his 'soul'. And do we not also find the ritual of confession in the form of talk shows and reality TV in which the celebrity is encouraged to 'reveal all'; and, even more commonly, in the mass confessional space of social media, in which ordinary people, without any encouragement at all, display their entire lives to the world, down to the most mundane and banal details? If anything, today there is such an excess of confessional behaviour, such an overexposure of the private to the public, that the very notion of the confession – that which reveals what is most hidden and intimate, and therefore what is supposedly most significant to the individual – has almost lost all meaning. The subject who now lives his life in the full gaze of the public – or what is imagined as its gaze – seems a strangely opaque figure, obscured by his own transparency.

The ritual of the confession is nevertheless central to modernity, for Foucault. Of course, this relates to his well-known thesis about sexuality: rather than sexuality being repressed in the modern era, on the contrary, we never cease talking about it and are always encouraged to talk about it – a confessional impulse that can be traced back to the codification of Christian penance in the thirteenth century (ibid., 58). Indeed, the injunction to confess the 'truth' of one's sexual desire as the inner secret of one's soul is key to Foucault's understanding of power as being positive and productive rather than repressive. The function of power is no longer primarily to prohibit, repress and censor, particularly not when it comes to knowledge of sexual desire. To imagine that sexual desire is repressed in modernity is to fall victim to the ruse of power, to the 'repressive hypothesis' (ibid., 17–49) that aims to convince us that there is a hidden truth of desire that is prohibited and that must therefore be liberated. Rather, power, as Foucault says, *produces* and *incites*: it produces a certain 'truth' of the subject as constructed around his sexuality, and it incites supposedly repressed pleasures and desires. In engaging in the ritual of confession, in confessing one's hidden sexual desires, one might imagine that one is on the side of freedom and liberation against power, but in reality one engages in a ritual of power and plays into the hands of a psychiatric–medical 'regime' that has, since the nineteenth century, demanded the production of knowledge about sexuality and seeks to classify and categorise desires and behaviours, pinning the individual to a particular identity. Even the practice of 'coming out' and revealing one's non-conforming sexuality or identity becomes part of the confessional machine and no longer poses a threat to power. As Foucault shows, even in the nineteenth century there was an obsession with revealing and cataloguing every conceivable sexual anomaly, 'a visible explosion of unorthodox sexualities' (ibid., 49). It is hard to tell whether there is any longer the same obsession with sex and its liberation that Foucault detected in the society around him, writing as he was in the aftermath of the movements of sexual liberation in the 1960s and 1970s. There seems today a new kind prudishness and moral puritanism, which we see in concerns around 'sexual harassment', for instance. Yet this may be simply the other side of the confessional society and 'the austere monarchy of sex' that Foucault believed was central to modernity (see ibid., 159).

As a genealogist, Foucault is interested in how the modern individual, as a confessing animal, was invented in early Christian cultures. Christianity invented the idea of a subject whose soul contained an essential secret that needed to be brought to light. Confession contains an avowal – such as 'I am sinful', 'I am a criminal', 'I am mad' – which has the effect of tying the individual to his own truth, changing his relationship to himself, as well as placing him within a power relationship where he comes under the authority of another (Foucault, 2014: 17). While practices of veridiction or 'truth telling' existed in pre-Christian, pagan cultures, it was only with Christianity that there emerged 'a hermeneutics of the self' – in other words, the idea of a self whose internal life, whose thoughts, desires and secrets must be examined and interpreted. What makes Christian veridiction uniquely different, according to Foucault, is that it imposes on the subject an obligation not only to follow the truth of religious dogma and revelation, but also to acknowledge and reveal the essential 'truth' about oneself:

> Christianity has bound the individual to the obligation to search for a certain secret deep within himself and in spite of everything that might hide this truth – a certain secret that, when brought into the light of day and manifested, must play a decisive role in his path towards salvation. (Ibid., 92)

Through practices of penance and baptism as forms of self-mortification and purification in early Christianity – particularly in the writings of the theologian Tertullian – through notions of obedience and spiritual direction that were part of monastic life and right through to the institutionalisation of the confession in the church as part of the ritual of sacrament, the idea developed of a subject who must manifest the inner truth of his sin.

The confession has to be seen as a technology of power, a form of conducting or governing through truth – a technique that finds its way, through the Christian pastorate, into modern governing apparatuses, becoming a key instrument of judicial, psychiatric, medical and penal power. As we have seen, government, for Foucault, is the 'conduct of conduct', and this operates not only through globalising strategies of the management and regulation of populations but also through the production of individual subjects who seek out their truth in the codes of power, and whose behaviour can therefore be conducted and guided in certain directions. Today we see that conduction is orchestrated not only by institutions, but by the computerised algorithms that collect data on the individual's internet browsing history and online purchasing, forming profiles through which he is guided towards particular products and even political choices. Whether the confession is made to one's priest or psychiatrist, whether one's secret truth is prised from the individual in a judicial or medical setting or offered freely online to the anonymous screen of the internet, upon which so much of our desire is projected today, the point is that the confession has become the main technique of individualisation, in other words of the production of the subject as an 'individual' (Foucault, 1978: 58–69). The individual and the state are not opposed concepts, but simply two sides of the same structure of a governmental power. For Foucault, then,

> Maybe the target nowadays is not to discover what we are but to refuse what we are ... The conclusion would be that the political, ethical, social, philosophical problem of our days is not to try to liberate the individual from the state, and from the state's institutions, but to liberate both from the state and from the type of individualization linked to the state. We have to promote new forms of subjectivity through the refusal of this kind of individuality that has been imposed on us for several centuries. (Foucault, 2002c: 336)

The Ethics of Subjectivation

What does it mean to 'refuse what we are'? What does Foucault have in mind when he talks about promoting new forms of subjectivity through the refusal of individualisation? Foucault offers us a genealogy of political theology that differs from Schmitt's not only in its focus on religious practices and institutions rather than on theological concepts, but also in the sense that it makes the subject, rather than the sovereign state, the main nexus of the politico-theological problematic. The subject and its relation to the regimes of truth that constitute him become the threshold and means of investigating the translation of religious practices and institutions into the secular social and political domain, as well as the site for any possible resistance to the techniques of pastoral power. The 'subject' therefore has a twofold significance for Foucault, as one who experiences 'subjection' (*assujettissement*) to power – in other words, turned into a governable subject – and as one who engages in alternative practices and forms of 'subjectivation' as a way of escaping or transforming his relation to power. 'Refusing what we are' means refusing to be identified in a particular, prescribed way, and reinventing ourselves in ways that allow a greater degree of autonomy. Like Stirner, who was engaged in a similar revolt against the pastoral power that lingered on in liberal humanism, Foucault is interested in the ways in which the subject might evade the 'fixed ideas' and essential identities that he was required to embody and conform to.[2] Both thinkers would be sceptical of any kind of politics based on 'identity'. Rather the aim of politics was to free the subject from 'identities' and to enable him to experience himself in new ways. Foucault's later studies of the pre-Christian pagan cultures of self-formation or *askēsis* ('exercise', 'training'), particularly in ancient Greece and Rome, give us glimpses of alternative ways of relating to oneself and to others, examples that, while not necessarily to be emulated – they have their specific historical time and place – reveal the possibility that always exists for doing things differently.

Before the transformation, under Christianity, of self-knowledge into a kind of self-mortification and self-renunciation, there existed an entirely different way of relating to oneself that took the form of care – the 'care for the self' (*epimeleia heautou*): 'You must attend to yourself, you must not forget yourself, you must take care of yourself. The rule "know yourself" appears and is formulated within and at the forefront of this care' (Foucault, 2005: 5). This consisted of a set of attitudes, behaviours, meditation, spiritual exercises, ascetic practices and forms of self-discipline through which one attended to oneself, reflected on one's thoughts and took responsibility for one's actions. It involved a kind of ethical and spiritual transformation of oneself. Indeed, as Foucault argues, the care of the self was one of the main forms of spirituality to develop in the ancient world, if one understands spirituality as a work 'of the self on the self' in order to find truth (ibid., 16). Importantly, this is quite different from theology, which implies, as we have seen, obedience to the truth of revelation, without the work of self-transformation central to spirituality. These are approaches to truth that are in many ways opposed – and, indeed, Foucault claims that the major conflict running through the history of Christianity was not between spirituality and science, as we might think, but between spirituality and theology (ibid., 27). I will return to this question of spirituality, as it contains important and untapped political resources.

While one might be tempted to think that care of oneself as a form of spirituality implied a selfish and narcissistic individualism or a solipsistic withdrawal into oneself, Foucault shows that, on the contrary, it implied very strict forms of self-discipline, as well as an ethical concern with one's relations with others, particularly in erotic, pedagogical and political relationships. Here the governing of others is fundamentally linked with the governing of oneself: if the subject was not able to master himself, to govern his own passions and appetites, particularly his appetite for power, then he was not able to effectively govern others, as the problematic figure of the tyrant in Greek philosophy shows.[3] For Foucault (2005: 252), then, the question of power relations is necessarily connected, as an ethical problem, with the relationship one has to oneself.

We find a similar kind of ethico-political concern in Foucault's other main example of subjectivation – *parrēsia*, or free and fearless speech. In contrast to confession, *parrēsia* imposed upon oneself a different kind of obligation to speak the truth, particularly when one was counselling others. What gave *parrēsia* its ethical quality was that it involved an element of risk and therefore of courage: the parrhesiast often spoke the truth at great personal risk, as Plato did when he gave unwelcome philosophical counsel to Dionysius, the tyrant of Syracuse (see Foucault, 2010b: 48–9). The personal risk taken by the parrhesiast is what commits him ethically to the truth of his words. *Parrēsia* is therefore always a challenge to power; it is combative, and it stages a kind of risky confrontation between truth and power. Importantly, the parrhesiast is one who is prepared to go against the opinion of the majority and to speak a singular truth against the *dēmos*, thus introducing a confrontation between the ethics of truth and the democratic will that became particularly acute in the classical age of Greece with the condemning to death of Socrates by the Athenian democracy. While democracy is necessary for there to be *parrēsia* – in the sense that it gives everyone an equal right to speak (*isēgoria*) and to exercise power – it also poses a threat to *parrēsia* when the democratic will becomes intolerant of dissenting voices (Foucault, 2010b: 48–9). *Parrēsia* is therefore precisely the problem of government; if democracies are to be governed well, if democratic decision-making is to be guided effectively, then it must be exposed to the ordeal of truth, to a principle that is always different from it and that is, at times, in an antagonistic relationship to the democratic will.

Are we seeing today a similar crisis of *parrēsia* within democracy? During the debate in the run-up to the EU referendum in the United Kingdom in 2016, a Conservative politician and campaigner for the Leave vote said, in response to the warnings of many economists about the damaging consequences of leaving the EU, 'The people have had enough of experts' – a remark reminiscent of the infamous declaration allegedly made by the judge who condemned the scientist Lavoisier during the French Revolutionary Terror: 'The Republic has no need of savants.' In other words, the *dēmos* had its own intrinsic wisdom and would decide without being influenced by 'expert' opinion. Similarly, in the United States, a president is elected who does not believe in climate change, against overwhelming scientific advice, and who withdraws the United States from a major global climate agreement. These are just two striking examples of a kind of democratic assault on truth telling in the form of scientific and technical expertise. This should be seen in the more general context of 'post-truth' politics as discussed in the previous chapter, where politicians can get away with the most outlandish and blatant lies, where they can invent 'alternative facts', without seeming to diminish their appeal; indeed, it often seems to make them more popular, as they can style themselves as speaking for ordinary people against the educated 'elites'. The situation has become, in a way, so hostile to expert opinion that, in April 2017, scientists around the world organised March for Science rallies to protest against the disdain for scientific evidence among politicians and policymakers. While, for Foucault, truth telling, as a philosophical and ethical practice, is different from technical knowledge,[4] it seems that today the scientific community, where it once occupied a certain position of symbolic and epistemological authority in society – in other words, it was on the side of power – now strangely takes up the position of the parrhesiast, as the dissident voice that speaks truth to power and protests against the disastrous sophistries that democracies seem to be encouraging.

Foucault's interest in *parrēsia* is more to do with its ethical dimension, as a way of relating to oneself and to others through the practice of truth telling. It is also a way of reflecting on the fraught relationship between philosophy and politics more generally, something I touched on in reference to Leo Strauss in the first chapter. Once again, while the philosopher might offer advice and counsel to those in power – as Plato tried to do, unsuccessfully, in Syracuse – the vocation of the philosopher and the vocation of the politician are different, even opposed, even though the domains of philosophy and politics exist in a certain relation to one another (Foucault, 2010b: 286). In Foucault's other example of *parrēsia*, the figure of the Cynic philosopher, there is an absolute confrontation between philosophy and politics. The Cynic philosopher – and Diogenes of Sinope is the main example – does not try to intercede in politics or advise the prince, but situates himself in a position of exteriority to society and signals, in the most scandalous manner possible, his contempt for society's laws and conventions. The Cynic practised *parrēsia* at the level of his daily life and sought to embody the courage of truth in his radical otherness, his asceticism and his militant rejection of social mores. The Cynics were the original anarchists; and, indeed, Foucault saw a parallel between ancient Cynicism and the revolutionary anarchism of the nineteenth century, in which there was a similar focus on bearing witness to one's life as a manifestation of the truth and purity of one's cause – a kind of revolutionary asceticism (Foucault, 2011: 184–5).

Counterconducts and Political Spirituality

While Foucault argues that these practices of subjectivation in pre-Christian cultures were different from the Christian hermeneutics of the self, which were focused on purification and obedience and took on more institutionalised forms, we must at the same time be careful about drawing too clear a division here. Many of the ascetic practices and modes of self-discipline associated with pagan ascesis found their way, in a different format, into Christianity, particularly in forms of asceticism among the martyrs of early Christianity and in the heretical movements of the Middle Ages. Like the Cynics many centuries before, these individuals and movements also practised poverty and asceticism and embodied a militant rejection of the institutions of their time, particularly those of the church, which is why they were savagely repressed. As Foucault (2011: 183) says, '[t]here is a Christian Cynicism, an anti-institutional Cynicism, a Cynicism that I would say was anti-ecclesiastical'.

It is would be wrong, then, to think that Foucault rejects the Christian tradition altogether. On the contrary, Christian ascetic practices, going back to its very early years, became an important source of resistance to the growing institutionalisation of church power. As we have seen, the central conflict within Christianity was between spirituality and theology and between ascetic practices and the pastoral power. In fact, during its history, the Christian pastorate experienced a crisis of government, with the explosion of what Foucault calls 'counterconducts' or forms of resistance against its power to conduct the lives of its members. The heretical movements during the Middle Ages – the Anabaptists, Hussites, Waldensians, Taborites, Cathars, Beghards, Beguines and so on – can be seen as anti-pastoral struggles in this sense (Foucault, 2007: 204). According to Foucault, Christian 'counterconducts' took a number of forms:

asceticism, which, as in the ancient practice, was a form of egoistic self-mastery intended to gain greater autonomy and to break with the relation of obedience; the formation of new, alternative *communities*, in which there was a refusal of church practices of baptism and confession and a rejection of special privileges for the pastor, as well as radical forms of equality and the rejection of private property; *mysticism*, which rejected church teaching and centred rather on the mystical experience and the soul's direct, secret, inner dialogue with God;[5] the *return to Scripture* as a way of bypassing the church's theological interpretation; and, lastly, *eschatological beliefs*, the idea of the fulfilment of time and the promised return of God as the true shepherd, which made the role of the pastoral shepherd redundant (see ibid., 204–14). All these beliefs, narratives and practices were, as Foucault shows, ways of counteracting and negating the authority of the pastorate and of disrupting its governing practices by constructing alternative ways of relating to oneself and to others. These practices, moreover, are marginal rather than central to the Christian tradition and can be seen as a renewal and rearticulation of more ancient practices of ascesis and care of the self. They might also be seen, I would argue, as forms of anarchist practice – a kind of spiritual anarchism, which sought to radically reorganise life autonomously and beyond the control of the church and the state, and which presented a genuine counterpoint to the political theology. The doctrine of the Free Spirit, for instance, was one of the more radical heretical movements of the thirteenth and fourteenth centuries: it preached egalitarianism, individual freedom, sensual pleasure and oneness with God and rejected the very idea of sin.

Foucault's study of 'revolts against conduct' that emerged in opposition to the pastorate might be seen in terms of a broader notion of 'political spirituality' that went beyond the Christian tradition and could be witnessed in more recent times. Foucault's other famous example here is the Iranian Revolution of 1978–9, which drew on the theological resources of Shia Islam to develop a synthesis of spirituality and political militancy. Foucault's interest in this event, which he witnessed first hand,[6] was in the forms of political, ethical and religious subjectivation it made possible, rather than in its strategic outcomes and achievements (see Foucault, 2002b). Just like the revolts in Christianity, the Iranian Revolution was as much a spiritual as a political uprising, seeing itself as taking place on an eschatological horizon that enabled people to risk their lives in revolt rather than submit to power:

> They inscribed their humiliations, their hatred of the regime, and their resolve to overthrow it at the boundaries of heaven and earth, in an envisioned history that was religious just as much as it was political. They confronted the Pahlavis [the Shah and his regime], in a contest where everyone's life was on the line, but where it was also a matter of millennial sacrifices and promises. (Foucault, 2002b: 450)

The Iranian Revolution, which is the global event that forms the backdrop to Foucault's interest in the pastoral power of government and the revolt against it, could be interpreted in terms of the conflict between political spirituality and political theology. This was, first, in the religious dramaturgy of the revolution itself, in which there was, as Foucault put it, a 'joust' between the figures of the king, in the form of the shah with his command of the army and the police, and the saint, in the form of Ayatollah Khomeini, the unarmed exile acclaimed by the people (Foucault, in Afary and Anderson, 2005: 203–9). Secondly, this conflict could be found, in an almost reversed way, in the gulf that Foucault later saw between the spirituality of the revolt itself and the political ambitions of the clerics who used the revolution to establish a new Islamic state based on religious orthodoxy: 'The spirituality which had meaning for those who went to their deaths has no common measure with the bloody government of an integrist clergy' (Foucault, 2002b: 451). Whether or not Foucault was naïve to try to separate one from the other, or to not foresee the ambiguous outcome of the revolution and its deterioration into an Islamic theocracy,[7] the important point, from our perspective, is the way in which religion – at least in its spiritual dimension – can provide resources, in the form of practices, concepts, metaphors, modes of experience, not only for the establishment of political authority but for the revolt against it. In other words, the mixing of religion and politics can not only sanctify power but also stimulate disobedience:

> the idea that the more men are concerned for their salvation in the hereafter the easier it is to govern them down here on earth does not seem to me to be in proper accord with a number of little things we are familiar with in the ancient or recent history of relations between revolution and religion. (Foucault, 2010b: 75)

The relationship between religion and politics is therefore a complex one. Religion can at times be on the side of political power and, at other times, be radically opposed to it. Today we are seeing this ambiguity play out in many guises, in Islamic fundamentalist and evangelical Christian movements opposed to the secular state but aspiring to replace it with their own theocratic version of the state; in the persecution, both by secular and theocratic states and by quasi-states, of religious minorities and non-believers; in the fracturing of societies along the lines of religion or competing views about the appropriate relationship between religion and politics; in the growing prominence of religious spirituality in some progressive social movements; as well as in what I see as a kind of secular spiritualisation, in the form of declarations of moral outrage, of the discourses of many protest movements. All these conflicts, movements and forms of political expression take place on an apocalyptic horizon abandoned by the great secular projects of progress and emancipation that characterised the twentieth century.

The challenge for us today, in the light of Foucault's genealogies – which are, after all, intended to disrupt the settled status of our present – is not simply to understand the religious roots of secular power; nor is it simply to prise apart religion and politics, something that can also have extremely dangerous consequences. Rather it is to identify and foster new forms of counterconduct, new ascetic practices, new modes of ethical subjectivation, whether religious or non-religious, which, like the Cynics of old, open up possibilities for an 'other life' and an 'other world'.[8]

6

Economic Theology

In his lectures on modern liberalism and neoliberalism, Foucault (2010a) showed how the market increasingly functions as the main site of veridiction or 'truth telling', passing judgement on the competency of the state. The penetration of the nation state by global markets generates, as we see, an at times conflicting relationship between economic and political sources of authority. Yet, while these poles appear to be opposed, they are simply different aspects of the empty place of transcendence left vacant by the collapse of the theological world. In seeking to occupy this once sacred place sometimes as allies, sometimes as rivals, it is no surprise that economic sovereignty and political sovereignty seem to take on theological hues. In this sense, rather than abandoning the problematic of political theology, we should supplement it with the notion of *economic theology*. While economic theology is a theology of immanence rather than transcendence – in other words, it is a theology coextensive with society rather than standing above it, as a separate entity – it shares with political theology a claim to the sacred, to an absolute order of truth, to being an indispensable condition our existence.

My argument in this chapter will be that, just as the problem of political theology arises with secularisation, the problem of economic theology refers to the way in which theological concepts and religious practices and behaviours were translated and incorporated into a secular economic rationality. Of course, Max Weber's thesis about the 'spirit' of capitalism as a secularisation of 'inner-worldly' Protestant asceticism is crucial here. However, the secularisation thesis needs to be supplemented by a genealogy of the idea of economy that goes back much earlier than the Reformation, to the patristic era of early Christianity. I also want to see capitalism today as part of the broader problem of the reign of technics. If there is such a thing as metaphysics today, it lies in the reign of technology over our lives, a process of domination accelerated under global capitalism.

Faith and Finance

When, in the wake of the 2007–8 global financial crisis, religious leaders condemned the greed, excess and irresponsibility of the banking industry, they touched upon an ambiguous relationship that has long existed between Christian theology and the market. As Cardinal Cormac Murphy-O'Connor said in his sermon in Westminster Cathedral in 2008,

> Christianity neither condemns nor canonises the market economy – it may be an essential element in the conduct of human affairs ... But we have to remember that it is a system governed by people, not some blind force like gravity ... Those who operate the market have an obligation to act in ways that promote the common good, not just in ways that promote the interests of certain groups. (Moore, 2008)

For the most part, Christian theology is not necessarily opposed to the idea of the market, but believes that it should be tempered by morality and guided towards the common good. The notion of the common good emerged in the Aristotelian tradition and was reflected in the thought of Aquinas, who claimed that the good of each individual was fundamentally connected to the good of others and dependent ultimately on God (see Hollenbach, 2004: 4). The notion of a higher good or general welfare took precedence over individual economic interests and emphasised the virtues of charity and moderation. In the gospels, moreover, worldly economic concerns are generally viewed as ephemeral in the context of the afterlife. Thus one is enjoined to 'sell your possessions and give to the poor' (Luke 12:33–4). We think also of the parable of the rich man and Lazarus (Luke 16), or the story of Jesus overturning the tables of the moneylenders in the temple (Matthew 21, Mark 11 and Luke 19), or the teaching about the difficulties a rich man faces in entering the kingdom of heaven (Matthew 19). At the same time, of course, these teachings were often belied in practice – we cannot ignore the historical links between the church and capitalism and the accommodations made in the Middle Ages by the church to the activities of the banks, despite its ban on usury. Moreover, the church's sale of indulgences as a financial remission of sin, against which Luther railed, operated as a kind of market of salvation.

The New Priests

However, my understanding of economic theology is to do less with the relationship that has existed historically between the altar and the counting house than with the way in which modern economics secularises certain theological concepts in its construction of the market and in its understanding of rational economic conduct. For instance, the idea of divine providence as developed in Augustine and Aquinas – which refers to God's ordering of the universe and his direct intervention in the world, often down to designing the tiniest details of creation – found its way into classical economic theory. Adam Smith's famous metaphor of the 'invisible hand', the market mechanism that mysteriously coordinates the individual pursuit of economic self-interest with the promotion of the common good, can be said to derive from this doctrine. The father of modern capitalism understood the world according to the laws of divine providence: 'As all the events in this world were conducted by the providence of a wise, powerful, and good God, we might be assured that whatever happened tended to the prosperity and perfection of the whole' (Smith, 1984: 274).

Perhaps, then, modern economics can be considered a secular theology. This is the view of economist Robert H. Nelson, who argues that the modern profession of economics is like a new priesthood. It has its own religious dogma, believes absolutely in its own fundamental truths, and has its arcane mysteries and rituals. While economists provide important technical knowledge and collect data on the economy, another of their roles, according to Nelson (2001: xv), 'is to serve as the priesthood of a modern secular religion of economic progress that serves many of the same functions in contemporary society as earlier Christian and other religions did in their time'. The economist's belief in rational progress as an article of faith is a form of secularised Christian eschatology.

However, to understand the implications of economic theology, we have to grasp not only the doctrinal nature of much economic thinking but, more importantly, the impact of certain forms of economic rationality on everyday life. Neoliberalism – as a governing rationality based on neoclassical economic theory – is of particular concern here, not only because it has, at least until recently, been dominant over the past three decades, but also because it promotes the marketisation of sectors of society and areas of life hitherto seen as part of the public domain. Whether it is in the fields of medical care, tertiary education, pension funds, energy and utilities, transport, welfare provision, vast areas of the state sector, and even prisons, few areas of life have escaped privatisation and marketisation. However, where neoliberalism as a form of economic (as well as political) theology has been particularly effective is in transforming the way we see ourselves. Not only must institutions be governed by the market, but the very soul of the individual must come to reflect this rationality. We see this, for instance, in the idea of 'human capital' developed by Chicago School economists, most notably Gary Becker. According to Becker, capital refers not only to external resources like money, shares, or factories and machines, but also to the skills, knowledge, health and levels of education that make up a person. When someone invests in his education, training or healthcare, one is investing in oneself as one's own stock of capital, just as one might buy shares on the stock market (Becker, 1993: 15–16). Thus the individual is turned into an 'entrepreneur of himself', as Foucault (2010a: 226–30) put it – as one's own enterprise. A person's capacities, qualities and characteristics become a source of current or future potential income; and, when one seeks to develop oneself physically, mentally, educationally – as our current culture of relentless self-improvement demands – one is investing in one's own capital. Thus capital becomes completely aligned with the human subject.

While the credibility of the neoliberal economic model might have been tarnished in the wake of the financial crisis – political discourse in many countries now turning against the idea of economic austerity and unlimited deregulation – neoliberalism as a *practice*, as a way of conducting one's life, has proven intractable because it has succeeded in colonialising the human subject. As a theology of immanence, it works more at the level of individual behaviours and practices than at the formal ideological level. Although the limitations of a neoliberal economic and political model are visible for all to see, it is very difficult to get away from the neoliberal way of life, from the view of ourselves as 'little enterprises'. This is something that fits in perfectly today with what has come to be known as the new 'Uber' or 'gig' economy, based on flexible, casualised labour. Here economic precarity becomes a 'liberation' from the traditional destiny of the career or the routine of full-time work: the individual, as his own enterprise, lives an 'autonomous' life, free to choose from a variety of different kinds of work, all available through an app on one's smartphone.

It is also through this theology of individual freedom that we might understand the ways in which neoliberal economics often intersects with religion. One thinks here, for instance, of the curious symbiotic relationship, particularly in the United States, between evangelical Christianity and aggressive forms of neoliberal capitalism (see also Connolly, 2005). Despite the seeming irreconcilability between socially conservative values based on religion and stable family life and the essentially amoral rationality of the market and individual self-interest, the 'conservative' political agenda has, if anything, grown stronger, more visceral, and more aligned in the US context: a major constituency of the pro-corporate, pro-free market Republican Party has been its Christian conservative base, which today enthusiastically supports Trump. One way to understand this phenomenon, beyond simply shared political expediency, is through the idea of neoliberal ascesis or work on the self – something that brings together spiritual transformation and economic self-promotion. Just as in the doctrine of human capital we are said to invest in ourselves economically, so for evangelical Christians there is a kind of spiritual self-investment, which is also an economic investment. We see this most explicitly in the phenomenon of televangelism – which started in the United States but has become global today – where self-styled preachers in their mega-churches tell their congregation that they can buy their salvation through donations or by purchasing books and other merchandise: the new form, it would seem, of the selling of indulgences. Perhaps the most striking example of this is what is known as 'prosperity theology' or 'prosperity gospel', which remains controversial among many Christian denominations[1] but has grown more prominent in recent decades. Joel Osteen, one of the foremost preachers of this purely capitalistic creed, counsels readers of his book *Your Best Life Now: 7 Steps to Living at Your Full Potential* on 'developing a prosperous mindset' as one of the 'most important aspects of seeing ourselves God's way' (Osteen, 2004: 82). We find here a new kind of individual ascesis, a new work of the self on the self, in which Christian theology is contrived to fit with the quest for greater personal wealth as a form of spiritual self-help.

Capitalism as Religion

In considering the strange nexus between theology and economics and between capitalism and Christianity, we can perhaps conclude that capitalism today has become a religion in itself. Perhaps capitalism can be seen a truly global religion, which draws on the energy and intensity of Christianity and other religions but at the same time secularises its theological categories and turns its impulses into the activities of profit making and endless consumption. According to Walter Benjamin (1996: 228–91), '[c]apitalism has developed as a parasite of Christianity in the West ... until it reached a point where Christianity's history is essentially that of its parasite – that is to say, of capitalism'. Perhaps our real religion today is consumerism, and our temples, churches and cathedrals are the shopping malls where we worship a more obscure god. If economists are the modern theologians, then capitalism is surely the modern religion. That this is a religion consisting of mundane practices and rituals such as working and shopping rather than a system of beliefs means that it is all the more internalised within the lives of its followers.

In his fragment 'Capitalism as Religion', Benjamin observes in capitalism several religious tendencies. He suggests that capitalism is a cultic religion, 'perhaps the most extreme that has ever existed' (Benjamin, 1996: 288–91). This is a cult without dogma and theology, in which utilitarianism itself takes on religious overtones. It is also a cult that is permanent and without reprieve: 'There are no "weekdays". There is no day that is not a feast day, in the terrible sense that all its pomp is unfolded before us; each day commands the utter fealty of each worshipper' (ibid., 288). Unlike other religions, whose worship is confined to certain sacred days or festivals, capitalism is an utterly mundane religion. Furthermore, this is a religion that generates ubiquitous guilt but, unlike other religions, without the possibility of atonement. But we can see the various ways capitalism generates guilt: one is made to feel guilty for being in debt, for never having enough, for not being able to conform to kinds of lifestyles and levels of consumption that capitalism promotes to us. The individual becomes, under capitalism, solely responsible for his own economic success or failure. This sense of the unrelenting burden of guilt without absolution is the reason why, for Benjamin, capitalism is a vast movement of despair.

Friedrich Nietzsche also noticed this connection between guilt and debt. In *On the Genealogy of Morals* he points out the similarity between the German words *Schuld* ('guilt') and *Schulden* ('debts'), showing how this originated in the earliest forms of the exchange and in the brutal punishments exacted by the creditor upon the debtor (Nietzsche, 1989: 62–3). Religion intensifies the relationship between guilt and debt. We come to feel increasingly indebted to a deity, who becomes our 'great creditor'. This reaches its high point with Christianity, which plays the cunning trick of turning our debt back onto the creditor, in the form of Christ's sacrifice on the cross:

> God sacrifices himself for the guilt of mankind, God makes payment to himself, God as the only being who can redeem man from what has become unredeemable for man himself – the creditor sacrifices himself for his debtor, out of *love* (can on credit that?), out of love for his debtor! (Ibid., 92)

Could there be a more effective way of making our debt and sense of guilt permanent than this act of sacrifice of the creditor on behalf of the debtor? The debt becomes immeasurable, something that is impossible to ever repay. Today, levels of household and personal indebtedness are at record highs: for instance, levels of credit card debt alone in the United States amount to $1 trillion, not including student loan and autocar debt (see Moyo, 2017). While this is no doubt creating the conditions for a future financial crisis on the same scale as, or possibly worse than, that of 2008, it also points to the way in which modern capitalism is increasingly based not so much on market exchanges between equals, but on the older, more hierarchical relationship between creditor and debtor, something that also corresponds to growing levels of wealth inequality. Yet it is always the indebted individual who is held morally accountable for this situation, just as one is held accountable in Christianity for original sin (see Lazzarato, 2012).

Marx, too, perceived a religious dimension to capitalism. Aside from the way in which religion functioned at certain times as an ideological prop to bourgeois domination, the very operation of the capitalist system had a religious structure, which could be seen particularly in the fetishistic nature of commodities: 'At first glance, a commodity seems a commonplace sort of thing, easily understood. Analysis shows, however, that it is a very queer thing indeed, full of metaphysical subtleties and theological niceties' (Marx, 1930: 43–4). According to Marx, under capitalism the commodity is transformed from a mundane object into a kind of sacred, transcendental, mystical thing, abstracted from its physical properties, its use value and the real social relations in which it was produced. The commodity obscures these social relations by reflecting them back to us in a commodified form, as if they were relations between things rather than relations between producers. By approaching the commodity as if it had an intrinsic value, one abstracts labour value into exchange value. In mystifying social relations in this way, commodities have a properly fetishistic character. In other words, it is by believing in the intrinsic value of the commodity – or rather by *acting as though* we believe in it – that relations of labour and social life in general can continue to be mediated through market exchanges. The commodity would seem to operate in exactly the same fetishistic way as sacred objects and religious relics: by acting as though they were endowed with sacred properties and mysterious powers, one perpetuates the religious illusion. Therefore, to understand the commodity, we must, as Marx says, 'enter the nebulous world of religion. In that world, the products of the human mind become independent shapes, endowed with lives of their own, and able to enter into relations with men and women' (ibid., 45).

Capitalism and Secularisation:
Weber and Protestantism

Marx claims, moreover, that, for a society where social relations between producers take a commodity form – in other
words, a bourgeois capitalist society – 'Christianity, with its
cult of the abstract human being, is the most suitable religion' (Marx, 1930: 53). Why should this be the case? Unlike
in earlier, precapitalist feudal times, where social relations
were much more interdependent and all had their fixed place
within a divinely ordained hierarchical order, modern bourgeois capitalism is based on the idea of the formally 'free'
individual, who is liberated from his social context and
engages, as an individual – rather than as a member of a
guild or association – in labour and commercial exchanges
as if he were a commodity on the marketplace. We have seen
this in its most extreme form in the idea of 'human capital'.
This abstract figure of the individual, removed from his
social setting, alone in the world and dependent only upon
himself, is one that is most reflective of Protestant Christianity. The Protestant Reformation in the sixteenth century did
not invent capitalism, but it invented its ideology – or, as
Max Weber put it, its 'spirit'.

In his essay *The Protestant Ethic and the Spirit of Capitalism*, Weber (2001) sought to understand the relationship
between Protestant spirituality and modern capitalism,
which required rational forms of conduct such as individual
utility maximisation and the calculation of profit. Why was
the greatest tendency towards economic rationalism exhib-
ited in the parts of Europe and among the sectors of society,
particularly the emerging entrepreneurial middle classes,
that were most influenced by Protestantism? According to
Weber, there was a relationship between a spiritual asceticism – found especially in Calvinism – and capitalist accu-
mulation. However, the values of enterprise, hard work,
astuteness and frugality that characterised the Calvinist
outlook were about more than simply the acquisition of
wealth. Rather they were part of a certain ascetic ethos, a

practice of moral discipline motivated by a sense of religious calling and duty rather than by greed. Indeed, the practice of wealth acquisition was deprived of any enjoyment. Self-discipline, hard work and austerity became ends in themselves – part of a quest for self-improvement, beyond any kind of utilitarian satisfaction:

> In fact, the *summum bonum* of this ethic, the earning of more and more money, combined with the strict avoidance of all spontaneous enjoyment of life, is above all completely devoid of any eudaemonistic, not to say hedonistic, admixture. It is thought of so purely as an end in itself, that from the point of view of the happiness of, or utility to, the single individual, it appears entirely transcendental and absolutely irrational. (Weber, 2001: 18)

How did this notion of profit-making as a calling develop? According to Weber, Protestantism, unlike earlier ascetic traditions, stressed the fulfilment of worldly duties rather than a monastic withdrawal from the world. Calvin emphasised the relationship between religious duty and worldly activity. The doctrine of predestination, wherein only some souls were destined to be saved by God's grace and others condemned, was turned by Calvinism into an impulse to engage in worldly activity as a way of fulfilling God's duties, as well as allaying one's religious anxieties. The Calvinist individual saw himself as a tool of God's will, and his engagement with the world, in the form of productive and useful activity, was a way of proving one's faith. So we have here a different kind of asceticism from that of the monks who shut themselves away in monasteries. The Protestant individual is, as it were, a monk *in* the world; asceticism went beyond the walls of the monasteries and church institutions and became engrained in social relations and in the individual conscience (ibid., 74). Thus, inner worldly devotion – where the individual's relationship with God was carried on in 'deep spiritual isolation' (ibid., 63) – went hand in hand with frenetic activity in the external word, particularly commercial activities. The

Protestant ethos, typified in Calvinism, is therefore one of salvation through good works and the deeply individualistic and capitalistic message that God helps those who help themselves.

Weber goes on to show how this inner-worldly asceticism, which at one level seems so irrational, becomes the impetus for a new, worldly rationalism that comes to characterise the 'spirit' of modern capitalism and produces a technocratic–commercial society full of 'specialists without spirit, sensualists without heart' (bid., 124). In incorporating and secularising this spiritual asceticism, modern capitalism ends up dispensing with it, no longer needing it once its work in reconstituting society had been done. The Protestant revolution, in liberating the individual from the bonds of the old theological order and in enshrining the spirit of individual enterprise in social relations, now succumbs to the world of economic rationalism and relentless commodification that it unleashed. According to Weber, '[s]ince asceticism undertook to remodel the world and to work out its ideals in the world, material goods have gained an increasing and finally an inexorable power over the lives of men as at no previous period in history' (ibid.). The modern culture of materialism is a far cry from that of Protestant asceticism, and those austere and religious Calvinist men and women would scarcely recognise themselves in today's figure of the modern consumer. However, perhaps there are traces of Protestant asceticism that linger still. Perhaps the idea of a duty to one's calling – which, according to Weber, 'prowls about in our lives like the ghost of dead religious beliefs' (ibid.) – still animates our lives and activity under modern capitalism, albeit in a different form.

The point I want to pick up on from Weber's account is the seemingly irrational aspect of religious asceticism, where frenetic activity no longer has any connection with the utilitarian satisfaction of human ends. Can we not see in our top CEOs and business leaders today a reflection of those Calvinist ascetics, whose hard work and relentless drive for profit was out of devotion to a calling, rather than serving any hedonistic purpose? Indeed, it is difficult to understand, at one level, the strange frenzy, the indomitable spirit that drives multibillionaire CEOs to work so hard, to devote themselves so utterly and single-mindedly to their work, to the sacrifice of everything else; why do they not simply enjoy the vast fortunes they have accumulated? It was reported, for instance, that the CEO of Tesla and Space X, Elon Musk, who has ambitions for the colonisation of Mars, works up to 100 hours a week (see Rodionova, 2016). Who knows what obscure gods these men of technology and commerce are worshipping, with their ascetic regimes, their frenetic hyperactivity, their pharaonic projects, their messianic ambitions of saving mankind. Who knows what strange gods we all serve when we work and consume seemingly without end or purpose, and usually without enjoyment. Are we not all heirs to those Calvinist ascetics – not necessarily in their frugality, but in their adherence and excessive devotion to a calling without end or rational purpose? Yet, unlike the religious Protestant, we serve ends we cannot understand; we engage in the world – with all our restless energy and activity – without really understanding why. At the heart of modern capitalism, in all its excessive utilitarianism and rationalism, there is, it would seem, a deep irrationality (see also Stimilli, 2017). We buy products we do not need and that do not bring us any lasting satisfaction or happiness. What is it that induces us, for instance, to upgrade our technological gadgetry whenever the latest model comes out? How do we explain the infantile enthusiasm and almost religious mania that greets the launch of the latest iPhone? Today the figure of *homo consumericus* stands beside the older figure of *homo economicus*: they can be seen as two sides of the same kind of secularised religious 'spirit' that grips the modern subject under capitalism.

However, rather than abandon the notion of asceticism, we need to reinvent it. Perhaps we need to rethink the idea of classical ascesis that Foucault spoke of, as forms of exercise of the self upon the self, designed to master one's appetites and therefore increase one's autonomy. In other words, can we develop forms of ascetic conduct and self-discipline that at the same time resist the idea of a calling – whether it is a call to capitalistic devotion and self-sacrifice, or the call to consumption without end?

Divine Economy

Our investigations so far have highlighted the theological foundations of modern economic life. Yet, if the economy can be said to have a theological character, then can we also say that theology has, in turn, an economic character? For example, the central tenet of Christian revelation – God's plan for our salvation – obeys an economic logic. The notion of the economy of salvation, or divine economy, has an essentially capitalistic structure. God invests in our salvation – as we have seen, he even sacrifices his Son to this end – and we are supposed to repay our debt to him in the form of faith and good works. Central to Christian theology is a form of economic exchange. Catholic teaching refers to the 'Christian economy' and, furthermore, makes reference to the 'deposit of faith' (see 'Sacred Scripture', in Catechism of the Catholic Church, n.d.). Here economy refers to God's creation of the world and his management of everything within it.

Following on from Foucault's analysis, Giorgio Agamben shows that liberal government essentially takes the form of an economy – the management of individual conducts. But, rather than seeking the origins of this in the Christian pastorate of the Middle Ages, Agamben traces it back much further, to the Church Fathers of the earliest years of Christianity. According to Agamben, the main problem for early theologians like Hippolytus, Tertullian and Gregory of Nazianzus was how to reconcile the idea of the Trinity – the three distinct persons of Father, Son and the Holy Spirit – with the notion of God as a single divine substance. This became particularly acute in the context of the defence of church orthodoxy against the Gnostic and Arian heresies. Here the ancient Greek concept of *oikonomia*, the management or administration of the household (*oikos*), was translated in theological terms, as the 'divine plan of salvation' and the 'mystery of the economy', and deployed as a way of explaining the idea that God could be both three persons and one at the same time. The paradox is explained by Hippolytus in terms of a sort of division of labour between different entities, which is at the same time the expression of the will of a single divine unity: 'The Father gives the orders, the logos performs the work, and is revealed as Son, through whom belief is accorded to the Father. By a harmonious economy [*oikonomia sumphōnias*] the result is a single God' (Agamben, 2011: 39). The idea becomes a pivotal paradigm for understanding not only the Christian schema of divine providence and the salvation of humanity, but also its later 'secularisation' into an immanent praxis of government.

How does this logic of the economic government work? As Agamben shows, the use of the notion of the economy by the Church Fathers to get around the Trinitarian problem inadvertently introduced a split within God between the functions of being and acting (ibid., 53). According to the idea of divine economy, God no longer directly intervenes in the world, but governs it providentially, through his Son. God becomes like the king who 'reigns but does not govern', according to the maxim of Adolphe Thiers; which, for Foucault, became the way for understanding the transformation of the sovereign function in modernity, as it gives way to the new *raison d'état*. Thus a division emerges between theology and economics, transcendence and immanence, ontology and praxis, sovereignty and administration. However, Agamben's main point is that these seemingly separated elements are at the same time hinged together, as part of the same paradigm, just as two distinct natures can exist in Christ. They operate as the two sides of what Agamben refers to as the 'bipolar machine of government'. Just as divine government needs both God to rule, and his Son and a divine bureaucracy of angels to administrate, so too does the modern idea of government need its symbols of sovereign legitimacy, as well as its apparatuses of technical and economic administration (ibid., 276). Thus the notion of *oikonomia* allows us to relate political with economic theology. Like Foucault, then, Agamben opens up a broader understanding of political theology, which goes well beyond the sovereign-centric paradigm and forces us to take account of its necessary relationship to economic theology and the problem of government.

At the same time, while the economic–governmental pole might appear to be dominant in late modernity, the problem of sovereignty has not gone away. How might we understand the symbolic place of sovereign transcendence and the recurrent need for legitimation, in the context of the economic problem of government? For Agamben, this has its origins in the practice of liturgical acclamation in the church – the hymns and arcane rituals through which the glory of God was praised. The practice of acclamation could be traced back to pre-Christian times, when pagan emperors were lauded through shouts of praise from the crowd – a practice that, as Kantorowicz showed, was also important to the legitimation of modern fascist leaders (see Agamben, 2011: 192–3). We should also recall that the technique of direct acclamation by democracy was important to Schmitt's understanding of dictatorship, and seen as more legitimate as an expression of the will of the people than parliamentary democratic institutions. What specific form does acclamation take today; from where does sovereignty derive its glory, its symbolic and 'democratic' legitimation? Here Agamben makes an important observation: the contemporary form of acclamation or glory takes place through the media, which become a cipher of 'public opinion': 'Contemporary democracy is a democracy that is entirely founded upon glory, that is, on the efficacy of acclamation, multiplied and disseminated by the media beyond all imagination' (ibid., 255). It is hardly controversial to say that the media, with their inordinate influence on political debate, have been the major instrument for constituting 'public opinion' as a site for the symbolic legitimacy of sovereignty – so much so that they seem to have become, in liberal democratic societies, a political institution in itself.

However, it would seem that the traditional modes of acclamation and political legitimation are starting to lose their symbolic efficacy, a symptom of which is the proliferation of alternate forms of media, as well as attacks on 'fake news' by politicians. One way to understand this generalised breakdown of legitimation is through Agamben's curious claim that the bipolar economic machine of government is essentially 'anarchic' in its structure and operation:

> *The fracture between being and praxis, and the anarchic character of the divine* oikonomia *constitute the logical place in which the fundamental nexus that, in our culture, unites government and anarchy becomes comprehensible... Anarchy is what government must presuppose and assume as the origin from which it derives and, at the same time, as the destination toward which it is traveling.* (Ibid., 64)

How should we understand this enigmatic formulation? What does it mean to say that government and anarchy are united, and that divine anarchy is what allows government to function? Here we must understand the particular way Agamben is using the word 'anarchy', as 'without *archē*' – in other words, without ontological foundation or governing rule. This, once again, goes back to the early theological debates over whether Christ the Son was founded on the Father or whether, like God, he is ungrounded. So, for Agamben, Christ's sphere of divine *oikonomia* – and the biopolar governmental machine on which it is based – is anarchic in the sense that it is not grounded in any preexisting rule or form of authority. Moreover, anarchy is what this machine presupposes in order to operate: government implies the ability to order the world, to impose a certain order where there was none before – as well as operating through the 'anarchic' structure of the market. However, this economic–governmental machine is essentially blind and without direction. There is, as Agamben put it, an empty throne behind the veils of power (ibid., xiii), a God who reigns but does not govern, and is therefore absent from the world. This is how we should think of the empty place of transcendence, the void left vacant by God, around which, I have suggested, the problems of political and economic theology circulate. The world today seems to be heading towards a general state of catastrophe, with one crisis piling on top of another: terrorist attacks, wars, civil strife, social division, economic dislocation, resource depletion and the constant prospect of ecological disaster. We get the distinct impression that today, despite the posturing of our little sovereigns, there is actually *no one* in charge, no directing force at the helm, and that the world is governed by a blind and nihilistic machine that, as it tries to impose order, only creates more anarchy and disorder. No wonder the anarchists like Proudhon used to say that anarchy is order, government is civil war. Of course, here the idea of anarchy is reversed to mean a harmonious self-managed social order that governments, which are anarchic in the 'bad' sense, disrupt.

If Agamben is right, however, and the governmental machine is heading towards anarchy and taking the world with it, then perhaps we need to rethink the notion of anarchy – or anarchism – to extricate it from the anarchic–governmental paradigm in which it becomes simply the nexus or threshold between order and disorder. An alternative understanding of anarchy is what Agamben is getting at when he says: '*This does not mean that, beyond government and anarchy, it is not possible to think an Ungovernable [un Ingovernabile], that is, something that could never assume the form of an oikonomia*' (ibid., 65). However, to do this requires something that is missing from Agamben's thought – a reconsideration of the anarchist tradition. This is something I will come to in the final chapter.

The Reign of Technics

The economic–governmental machine that Agamben analyses can be seen as part of an even more pervasive machine

– that of technics. By technics I am referring not only to actual machines and technology, but to a certain mode of activity and a rationalisation of life that comes with the technological age. The mechanised clock in the fifteenth century, the steam engine and spinning jenny in the eighteenth century, the locomotive and internal combustion engine in the nineteenth century, the Fordist assembly line and computing technology in the twentieth century, and the internet and artificial intelligence in the twenty-first century – all these inventions not only have allowed the development of modern capitalism, but have contributed to a 'machine culture' in which work and life are increasingly organised in a technical way around the operation of the machine.

The culture – or, as I would put it, the cult – of technology is something that is not entirely reducible to capitalism; rather it is something that encompasses capitalism, but also raises a broader set of questions and concerns about the social and natural environment and the very status and meaning of human activity. Writing in the late 1940s, Jacques Ellul warned of the consequences of the technological society, in which technique, which we imagine to be under human control and at the service of human ends, develops according to its own autonomous rationality and would come to displace and dominate human activity. There would be a total integration of human, and even spiritual life into technique – a new kind of totalitarianism. Here Ellul points to a kind of technical theology in which technique's secularisation of the religious and spiritual disposition ends up in a new form of religious mysticism:

> Technique fully satisfies the mystic will to possess and dominate. It is unnecessary to evoke spiritual powers when machines give much better results. But technique also encourages and develops mystical phenomena. It promotes the indispensable alienation from the self necessary, for example, for the identification of the individual with an ideology. (Ellul, 1964: 422–3)

In displacing traditional forms of mystical and religious spirituality – in incorporating these into itself – technique comes to occupy its place of transcendence and becomes the new site of the sacred, the new source of charismatic and mystical authority in society. The 'ecstatic phenomena' that Ellul refers to, the manifestations of a renewed religiosity in modern secular societies, which he believes will only increase in frequency and intensity, are a sign of 'the subjection of mankind's new religious life to technique' (ibid., 423). A similar point has been made by Jacques Derrida, who points to the relationship between 'technocapitalism' and renewed and often violent forms of religious fundamentalism in (post) secular modernity (Derrida, 1998: 1–78; see also Suarez-Villa, 2009). This theological dimension of the culture of technics was also observed by historian of technology Lewis Mumford, who commented on modernity's absolute faith in the machine: 'Only as a religion can one explain the compulsive nature of the urge towards technological development without regard for the actual outcome of the development of human relations themselves' (Mumford, 1934: 365).

Writing in the 1930s, Mumford believed that our faith in technology, which had been so dominant over the past two hundred years, would break down as we became aware of the dangerous uses to which the machine was being increasingly put. Today, however, it seems that, if anything, the very opposite is happening. While there is perhaps a certain awareness of the excesses of technology – here the church has been particularly critical of aspects of bioscientific research, for instance into the cloning of genes – there is no overall sign that the technological religion is waning. On the contrary, our lives are now almost totally saturated by technology, to the point where most social activities, interactions, and relationships, whether at work or at home, whether in the private or public space, from the most mundane to the most intimate, are conducted through the medium of technology and become increasingly virtualised and abstracted. The postindustrial or information age, which is based on astonishing advances in computer technology, has meant a profound integration of the human subject into pervasive networks of communication and data. The development and continual enhancement of smartphone technology means that we spend more time 'plugged in' to social media and online content than not. The average adult in the United Kingdom now spends about nine hours a day on online social media, longer than he or she would spend sleeping. The obsession with seamless communication has produced a world of hyperconnectivity from which there is little escape. According to a former product manager at Google, big internet platforms and social media companies have 'hijacked' the human mind and manipulated human behaviour, creating a kind of cognitive dissonance whereby we are continuously distracted and drawn in by stimuli and information, so that we spend more and more time online (see Thompson, 2017). The world of hyperconnectivity has the potential to function as a tool of total surveillance and control. The 'utopia' of the 'internet of things' (IoT) – enthused over by our Silicon Valley messiahs – presents a terrifying vision, in which all physical devices, whether home appliances, computers and smartphones, electronic and communication systems, are linked together in an online network. The individual in this cybernetic hell becomes simply a node in a network and, moreover, comes to see himself in this way. The neoliberal subject, *homo economicus*, the acquisitive, entrepreneurial, utility-maximising individual, is now accompanied by *homo connectus*, the constantly connected, constantly trackable individual. Some time ago now, Gilles Deleuze diagnosed the emergence of 'societies of control', in which new techniques of control, based on computers and information technology, were replacing the older disciplinary institutions (Deleuze, 1992: 3–7). And yet, as we see today, this immersion into overlapping networks of surveillance and control takes place without any coercion whatsoever, as people, in the name of convenience or technological novelty, willingly purchase the instruments of their own enslavement. They store their personal information on 'the cloud', connect themselves to smartphone apps that monitor their behaviour and health, or even allow themselves to be micro-chipped by their employers. With this new digital voluntary servitude, the very interiority of the body and the psyche are colonised, turned inside out, by the machine.

How else do we explain this behaviour other than by saying that we are apparently in the grip of a kind of religious enthusiasm, or even a religious psychosis? We worship the technological god, seek our salvation in it and believe that it can improve our lives and solve the problems of the world. Our daily practices and habits of obsessively checking social media on our smartphone, with the same ritualised dedication with which a devout Catholic might count on his rosaries, point to a new form of religious neurosis. Benjamin suggested that the main mental illness of the new capitalist religion was anxiety or 'worries'; but can we not also attribute the growing prevalence of anxiety, not to mention depression, to the technological religion that seems to encourage such obsessive behaviour? Many studies today suggest that technology and our constant exposure to online communication and social media increase anxiety and depression.[2] We now talk about smartphone and social media addiction, and people describe the sense of panic they often feel when they are disconnected from their devices. Communicative technology seems to be producing a kind of generalised attention deficit disorder where we find it increasingly difficult to concentrate on one piece of news or information for more than a few seconds, as we are constantly bombarded with other stimuli competing for our attention. This might also be an explanation for the suicidal drives and murderous impulses that are so much in evidence today (see Berardi, 2009) – a kind of apocalyptic or nihilistic sensibility that also takes political form in aggressive identitarianism, which, in the case of the so-called alt-right, for instance, also finds its forum on the internet.

So how do we begin even to grasp, ethically and politically, the implications of the technological, technocapitalist age that we now live in – an age in which automation will displace vast sectors of humanity's workforce, in which we now seriously contemplate a future of sexual and romantic relationships with robots, and in which we speculate on the threat to the autonomy and identity of the human posed by artificial intelligence? (See also Habermas, 2003.) However, what has come to be known as the posthuman or transhuman condition, in which the meaning of the human is fundamentally transformed by new technologies, has to be seen as only an extension of the humanist religion that Stirner analysed. The fantasy of the machine-man goes back to the scientific age of the seventeenth century, with the metaphors of man as automaton that we find in Descartes and Hobbes or in the eighteenth-century physician, philosopher and former student of theology de La Mettrie (1996), who described the workings of *l'homme machine*. The figure of Man who, for Stirner, has replaced God and has taken on his divine power, now becomes conjoined with technology to create a kind of new prosthetic or cyber-God, technologically enhanced, plugged in to networks, both master and servant of the technological world he has created.

To break down this economic–technical–theological machine – whose operation also intensifies the problematic of political theology – and to bring it back under human control, we can no longer rely on the categories of secular humanism. Or, rather, we must seriously reconsider these philosophical categories in light of the age of the Anthropocene, in which the impact of human activity, the obsession with economic growth, and the relentless development of technology have now fundamentally and irreversibly transformed the Earth's atmosphere and ecosystem. We must also develop new profane practices – indeed a new profane approach to the world. And it is to this task that I turn in the following, and final, chapter.

7

Conclusion

The Politics of the Profane

My overall thesis has been that political theology – as the problem of political legitimacy and foundation – emerges as a specific response to secularisation and constitutes itself around the place of transcendence left vacant by theology in the modern era. Modern forms of political and economic power seek to occupy this space and to incorporate its sacred dimension. In displacing religion in this way, modern power secularises itself and at the same time becomes divine and transcendent. Thus, as we have seen, the idea of political sovereignty is modelled on the transcendence of God and his authority over the world. And even economic and techno-logical power – which should be understood in terms of a theology of immanence rather than of transcendence – nevertheless assume the status of an absolute truth, akin to religious revelation. The problem of political and economic theology is less about the modern power of religion – with which it nevertheless continues to be intertwined – and more about the modern religion of power.

How can we respond, then, to the problem of power? What resources are available to us today to put a stop to the politico-economic machine of power that is impelling us towards catastrophe? How might we think and act in ways that are no longer caught up in the dynamics of political theology? These are the questions that this chapter, by way of a conclusion, will address. My claim will be that it is in the notion of the profane that we can find some answers.

The Secular and the Sacred

As it will have been evident throughout the book, greater secularisation cannot be a sufficient response to the problem of political theology, simply because political theology itself is predicated on secularism. Of course, we must not discount the historical importance of secular institutions, the separation of church and state, and the idea of a public space, at least formally free from the influence of religion. In consigning religion to the private realm, the process of secularisation freed us from the tyranny of church dogma and gave the individual a greater degree of choice over his own life and conscience. These are significant achievements and, while the formal secular political space might be weakened today, we should not be too hasty in welcoming the 'post-secular' condition, even if we are compelled at the same time to recognise its reality. My point, rather, is that secularism itself retains a certain theological impulse, a trace of the sacred, which is internalised within social structures and becomes the foundation for new forms of economic and political power that seek to fill the empty place of transcendence left over from religion.

The discussion so far has examined several important diagnoses of the theological dimension of modern secularism. Stirner showed us that modern secular humanism was simply a reinvention of Christianity and that the figure of Man was the new God. The decline of theological categories merely gave rise to a new world of moral and rational ideals and political institutions that became just as sacred, and had a similarly alienating and dominating power over life. In my discussion of the psychoanalytic theories of Freud and Lacan, I showed that the problem of the persistence of religion went even deeper: secularism meant only the entrenching of God within the structures of the unconscious; the removal of God from the external symbolic world became, paradoxically, the impetus not only for the revival of religion, but also for new forms of moral inhibition. Moreover, in my investigations into sovereignty, government, economics and technology, I showed how religious or divine power was translated into modern secular institutions and practices. Leviathan had become the new 'Mortall God', and government was a secularisation of the Christian pastorate. The modern subject was still a confessing animal, and *homo economicus* bore the visage of the ascetic Protestant. Modern practices of work, consumption and technological fetishism could be seen as secularised forms of religious devotion and ritual.

Jacques Ellul, whom I discussed in the previous chapter, identified the continuity of the sacred within secular society. While the formal power of religion had been displaced, modern secularism had unleashed new demons, new forms of sacred dogma and belief systems, whether in the reign of technology and scientific rationality or in new secular political religions. Indeed, the very forces of secularisation, or *desacralisation*, end up becoming sacred in turn (Ellul, 1975: 67). The reason for this, according to Ellul, is that the sacred provides an essential structure to all societies, whether secular or religious: the sacred is something that gives order to the world and provides us with a place within it. It integrates the individual into a collective through a shared reference to a transcendent (ibid., 54). That is why the dissolution of the sacred dimension through the process of secularisation ends up in the reconstitution of the sacred in different forms. We can understand the problem of political theology from this perspective as well: it is an expression of a desire for incarnation into a kind of transcendent political community, the sovereign state.

Furthermore, the return of the secular sacred follows a particular structural pattern of order and transgression. The two ordering poles of secular society are, according to Ellul, technology and the nation state, which, while they historically contributed towards desacralisation and the displacement of theology, have become in turn sacred, totalising ideas: technology 'more often arouses apocalyptic ecstasies or visions of the kingdom of God than rational reflection' (ibid., 74–5); and the nation state, a mystical communion of two ideas, is sacred in the sense that 'people accept it, live it and look upon it as the great ordainer, the supreme and inevitable providence' (ibid., 81). Yet, according to Ellul, we also engage in specific forms of transgression, in an attempt to desacralise these ideals. Sex becomes a way of breaking with our total, ecstatic integration into technology (although today – Ellul was writing in the 1970s – it would seem that sex has become more and more aligned with technology and therefore no longer has this transgressive power). Revolution is a way of desacralising and transgressing the nation state. However – and this is the crucial point – these forces of transgression themselves become sacralised. In an analysis that seems very close to Foucault's, Ellul shows how sex, in its association with liberation, becomes glorified and sacred, being accorded great importance in modern society. Meanwhile, revolution comes to be seen as a holy creed and a sacred duty of the zealot. It becomes a kind of religious festival, which, in seeking to capture the place of state power, only fetishises it and makes it sacred: 'The purpose is to reinstate it as a sacred and to incorporate oneself into it' (ibid., 86). I would argue that this dialectic between the sacred and transgression is at the heart of the mystery of political theology. Revolutions, whether political or even sexual, continually fall into the trap of the place of power, the empty place of transcendence around which political theology is constituted.

The Profane

If secular revolutions only confirm the sacred, then are we condemned to remaining within the politico-theological paradigm of sovereignty? There may be something in the notion of the profane that offers some clues here. For Ellul (1975: 48), the profane is always connected with, and predicated upon, the sacred – and is therefore something that can always be resacralised. Yet it is possible to understand the profane in a different way, which goes beyond the dialectic of the secular and the sacred.[1] The Latin word *profanus* meant literally 'before (or outside) the temple', and thus came to signify something that was unholy or not consecrated, something that could therefore not be admitted to the place of sacred rites. As Stirner showed, however, in the modern secular age, it was not the profane that threatened the sacred, but the sacred that threatened the profane: the new humanist religion saw an expansion of the temple walls to encompass the whole of society. We tend to associate the profane with secular but, as we see, the secular itself becomes a vehicle for the sacred.

Instead, we can define the profane in terms of a certain 'worldliness' that resists theological abstraction and transcendence and implies becoming and openness, and even a certain connectedness with the world. At the same time, my understanding of the profane should not be confused with materialism, which, as I have argued, is animated by another kind of spirit, another kind of rationality or inner truth, such as the unfolding of a dialectical process, or the historical laws that we find in Marxian revolutionary eschatology. Worldliness, on the contrary, embraces indeterminacy, contingency and multiplicity rather than the idea of a single, rational historical process.

The notion of the profane I am developing here, as a certain attitude of worldliness and becoming, implies also an ethos of care for what exists, and even remains open to the possibility of a certain 're-enchantment' of the world. If secularism is characterised by an experience of 'disenchantment' and yet results in a *re*sacralisation of its technical, scientific, economic and political forces, then perhaps the only way to counter this is through a respect for the multiform possibilities already present in the world, particularly in the natural world; a realisation of, and an openness to, our necessary entanglement with nature, with the natural ecosystems that form the true basis of our lives. A profane re-enchantment of the world does not mean a return to the theologically transcendent, but rather a recognition of our profound connection with, and dependency upon, complex systems and processes, particularly in the natural world, that we do not fully grasp; and even a naïve sense of wonderment and joy at the mysteries of nature, which we often cannot fathom. It is a recognition also of the fundamental limitations of the human condition, and a rejection of the hubristic humanism and anthropocentrism that not only have been the cause of such widespread environmental devastation and squandering of natural resources, but have led to our alienation from nature. Modernity's technologically enhanced humanist religion operates through the same categories of transcendence and the sacred as Christianity (or Judaism and Islam): just as God transcends and stands above man, man in turn transcends and stands above nature. There is an abstraction from the profane world and from the creatures, both human and non-human – a distinction that in any case we are increasingly forced to question today – who dwell within it. On the other hand, to understand the natural world in a profane way, as having its own meaning and significance beyond its mere utility to human ends, dislodges the politico-theological paradigm whereby life is sacrificed on the altar of abstraction.

Ecology and Theology

What role, if any, can theology play in our rethinking our relationship to the natural world? On the one hand, the Judeo-Christian tradition is at the root of the anthropocentric worldview, which sees the natural world and living things as existing only for the use and enjoyment of humanity. Did not God grant us dominion over 'the fish of the sea, and over the fowl of the air, and over every living thing that creepeth upon the earth'? Was mankind not commanded by God to 'fill the earth and subdue it' (Genesis 1:28)? With what terrible determination and at what appalling cost have we carried out God's commandments! The Earth has been filled and subdued to the point of exhaustion. Mined and plundered for resources, overfished and overgrazed, deforested and degraded, poisoned and polluted – the world is faced with the prospect of the collapse of the very ecological systems that sustain all life. The effect of human activity and consumption on our overpopulated planet has been the drastic depletion of natural resources and the extinction of countless animal species. Scientists now warn of the 'biological annihilation' as part of the sixth mass extinction event or 'Anthropocene extinction', whose rate far outstrips that of any other period in the Earth's history. The very fact that human activity has now fundamentally altered the ecological balance of the planet highlights the disastrous implications of a theological tradition that makes man the master of the Earth and lord of other species. As Lynn White (1967: 1203–7) claimed, Christianity was 'the most anthropocentric religion the world has seen'. Unlike the pagan world it displaced – in which natural objects and living creatures had a special spiritual significance and personality – Christianity introduced a dualism between man and nature that made it possible to objectify and exploit nature in 'a mood of indifference to the feelings of natural objects'.

At the same time, there are elements within the Christian tradition, particularly in some of its mystical and ascetic strands, that have been more hospitable to nature and have endowed all living things with significance. We think here, for example, of the story of St Francis of Assisi preaching to the birds, or of his amicable compact with a ferocious wolf, or of his compassion for the wild doves caught in the huntsman's net. In all these stories there is a kind of joy shared by all living creatures in creation – each living thing has an equal and unique place in the community of God. 'O Brother Leo, thou little lamb of God!', St Francis is reputed to have said,

> if the Friars Minor could speak with the tongues of angels;
> if they could explain the course of the stars; if they knew the
> virtues of all plants; if all the treasures of the earth were

revealed to them; if they were acquainted with the various qualities of all birds, of all fish, of all animals, of men, of trees, of stones, of roots, and of waters – write that this would not be perfect joy. (Uglino, n.d.: 24)

More recent Christian theology has sought to incorporate an ecological sensibility and to come to terms with the environmental crisis and its implications for the doctrine of creation. Indeed, it would seem that, when Christian theology seriously confronts ecological questions, it has to abandon, or at the very least radically revise, its more anthropomorphic tendencies. For instance, Protestant theologian Jürgen Moltmann, who develops an ecological doctrine of creation, has argued that, if the world is really God's creation, then it is also God's property, not man's. Humans can only be the stewards of the planet, which is on loan to them. Indeed, *theocentrism* – the idea that God is the centre of the universe – actually entails a rejection of crude anthropocentrism (Moltmann, 1985: 31). While humans might have a special place in creation, they must recognise the equal right and status of all living things as inhabitants of the house of God. This realisation leads us to no longer objectify the natural world, but to see it in a fundamentally different way: 'we begin to understand a life system in the light of its own special environment. Things are no longer merely objects for the human subject' (ibid., 37–38). This idea can also be found in some of the mystical tendencies of Judaism. Although Judaism is a largely anthropomorphic religion, the Kabbalistic tradition contains elements of a critique of anthropocentrism and can even accommodate the idea that non-human species are also a reflection of God's image (see Mevorach, 2015).

The encounter with ecology means, furthermore, that one can no longer hold on to the idea of a transcendent God who stands above and apart from the world. Rather, Moltmann talks about a God who is *immanent* in the world; a creator who is part of his own creation: 'The centre of this thinking is no longer the distinction between God and the world. The centre is the recognition of the presence of God *in* the world and the presence of the world *in* God' (Moltmann, 1985: 13). This view of God as present in his own creation has radical consequences for our own relationship with nature. Rather than seeing nature as a neutral object of exploitation and domination, we should identify with it, in its suffering and vulnerability, and see it as an enslaved creation that yearns for liberty (ibid., 39). Moltmann's notion of God's immanence in the world is actually very close to my own idea of the profane as 'worldliness' and contingency:

> Understanding nature as God's creation means seeing it as neither divine nor demonic, but viewing it as 'the world'. If this world has been *created* by God, then it is not necessarily existent; it is contingent. Its very being is contingent, and so is everything that happens in it. But if it is contingent, it cannot be deduced from the idea of God ... The rational order in which and through which we comprehend and know worldly happenings is therefore in itself contingent, temporal and open to change. (Ibid., 38)[2]

This sort of eco-theological approach, with its emphasis on mutual interpenetration over transcendence, complexity and dependency over independence, entails a rejection of political theology, which, as we know, is structured around a hierarchical and transcendent relationship of God to the world. Indeed, there is a clear link between political theology and anthropocentricism, between political domination and environmental domination. It is no surprise that our little despots today often show such contempt for the natural environment, seeing it only in terms of a commercially exploitable national resource. Ecology, on the other hand, implies a complexity, entanglement and mutual interdependence of life forms that is an anathema to sovereign power. Yet, if God does not stand transcendent over the world – if, on the contrary, God, human beings and the natural world form part of one living, interdependent entity – then there is no way one can sustain, at least from a theological perspective, the political concept of sovereign transcendence. This hierarchical relation is entirely dissolved and replaced with a much more egalitarian and reciprocal model of social and political relations – one that is closer to anarchism. Political theology, at least in the form that we are familiar with, breaks down in the face of ecological crisis. Just as man's domination over nature is no longer acceptable, neither is the sovereign state's domination over society.

Anarchism and Political Theology

The relationship between political and ecological domination has also been a focus of anarchist theory (e.g. Bookchin, 1982). Its uncompromising critique of political authority and its alternative, non-hierarchical vision of social relations – which can also include non-exploitative relations with nature – make anarchism essential to any understanding of profane politics. Moreover, the original meaning of anarchy as the absence of rule or foundation is another way of expressing the notions of ontological contingency, openness and relatedness to the world that I have associated with the profane. Anarchy is what resists transcendence and makes it impossible to establish hierarchies, whether of the metaphysical or of the political kind.[3] That is why, as I suggested earlier in the book, anarchism is really the counterpoint to Schmitt's theory of sovereignty and the necessary point of departure for any serious critique of political theology.

However, we must think carefully about the notion of anarchy, as it has a somewhat ambiguous, slippery relationship with political theology. As we saw, Schmitt's politico-theological apparatus of sovereignty is mobilised primarily against the threat posed by revolutionary anarchism, which he regards as his absolute enemy. However, as we also saw, sovereignty can only work effectively against this threat by becoming 'anarchic' itself, that is, by suspending the rule of law in the exception and becoming autonomous or auto-foundational. Anarchy and the exception are like two sides of a Mobius strip: in opposing each other, they find themselves on the same continuum, sharing the same structure – which is why it is difficult at times to distinguish between revolutions and counterrevolutions. This is also why, as we saw in the previous chapter, Agamben has pointed to the anarchic nature of power. Anarchy is the mystery at the heart of political theology. It is political theology's mortal enemy, what it disavows and fears most; yet anarchy is also what political theology must in a sense assimilate and imitate in order to neutralise its threat. In considering whether anarchism can be an effective critical response to political theology, we therefore need to take seriously Schmitt's curious and seemingly paradoxical charge against his anarchist adversaries, namely that Bakunin, 'the greatest anarchist of the nineteenth century, had become in theory the theologian of the antitheological and in practice the dictator of the anti-dictatorship' (Schmitt 2005: 66).

How should we understand this? Schmitt's point was that the anarchist shared with the counterrevolutionary an absolutist position on the sovereign state, to the point where they were like mirror images of each other. Moreover, Bakunin's absolutist rejection of the state may have led him at times to advocating 'invisible dictatorships' – although these were not dictatorships in the common sense, but more secretive, conspiratorial organisations of revolutionaries. However, where I think Bakunin does fall into the trap of political theology – the problematic that he was first to diagnose – was in the way he resorted to theological categories in his attack on theology: so extreme and unrelenting was his hatred of Christianity and the church that, as we saw, he invoked Satan in his war against God and the state. Bakunin's revolutionary 'Satanism' could correctly be regarded as an anti-theological theology, as could his celebration of immanence and materialism as a new kind of religion of life and humanity, which would come to supplant the old religions of transcendence.

The classical anarchism of the nineteenth century, of which Bakunin as well as Kropotkin were the foremost representatives, was a kind of secular revolutionary theology. Materialism was invoked against religion, immanent and biological life against the sacred and the transcendent, reason against superstition, science against religious dogma and obscurantism, humanity against power, and society against the state. The state was seen as the cold and unnatural monster that oppressed humanity and destroyed natural social relations. Yet it was the anarchists' implacable hostility to the state that in a way fetishised it and made it sacred. This at least is the view of Ellul (1975: 81): 'it [the state] was looked upon as the Beast of the Apocalypse, the focal point of all oppression. The frenzied anger of the anarchists towards the state, their blind vengeance against all its agents, shows the extent to which it was sacred to them.'

How, then, can anarchism escape this dialectic that we have identified between the secular and the sacred that perpetuates political theology? Or is radical politics condemned to reaffirming what it opposes, to resacralising what it seeks to desacralise? If anarchism is to contest the politico-theological paradigm, it must be able to escape the shadow of power, the shadow of the all-powerful sovereign state, or what Lacan would call 'the discourse of the Master', which holds it in such thralldom. By this I mean that the idea central to classical anarchism, of a revolution against state power, needs to be rethought. Anarchism is acutely aware, much more so than other radical philosophies, of the dangerous lures of power, which is why, unlike Marxists and Marxist–Leninists, who believed that the state apparatus could be used as an instrument of revolutionary transformation, anarchists urged that state power be destroyed as the first revolutionary act. However, it is not quite clear what the revolutionary destruction of state power would actually mean today, especially as the contours of state sovereignty have become much less distinct in the global age and power is no longer as centralised as it was in the nineteenth century. Nor is it clear what would replace the state, and indeed whether people would be ready to organise themselves cooperatively at a society-wide level. So, instead of imagining a kind of apocalyptic revolutionary event that would dislodge the excrescence of the state power and liberate society, it may be more productive today to think about practices of self-transformation – what we have referred to as ascesis – that enable us to modify our relations with others and with our immediate environment and to build different kinds of social organisations, which give us a greater degree of autonomy from state power. Central here is the idea of what might be called deinstituting practices, which are not simply anti-institutional, but depose the legitimacy of the state order by going around it rather than attacking it directly. Some clues may be gained here from Stirner's idea of the insurrection, which I discussed in a previous chapter, in which, as distinct from the revolution that only succeeds in creating institutions of a different kind, the individual works himself 'out of the established' and affirms himself in his indifference to power.

There is, paradoxically, something 'spiritual' about this particular political ethos I am describing – despite Stirner's undoubted protestations to the contrary. Indeed, it is very close to the position of Christian anarchism, which takes Christ's message of non-violence, as well as the indifference to power, as central. As a proponent of Christian anarchism, Ellul argues that, notwithstanding the anticlericalism of early anarchist movements and ideologies, there are important resonances between the two sets of ideas: if authority can only come from God, then this automatically de-delegitimises any claim to authority by political institutions like the state and releases us from our obligation to obey them. Christianity, if taken seriously, turns us into conscientious objectors to state authority and violence (see Ellul, 1991). In this way the paradigm of political theology is turned on its head. Rather than God's authority translating into sovereign authority, it completely undermines it; rather than identification with and obedience to Christ leading to political obedience, as Schmitt would have it, it leads to anarchy. However, the central insight of Christian anarchism is the idea that Jesus did not oppose political power – he said, after all, that we should render unto Caesar what is Caesar's – but rather regarded it with disdain. The interpretation of Christ's message offered by Ellul is that, if power corrupts, we should not necessarily try to overthrow it, as this only confirms our enthrallment to it, but should create alternative social structures and practices: 'In other words, do not be so concerned about fighting kings. Let them be. Set up a marginal society which will not be interested in such things, in which there will be no power, authority, or hierarchy.' Moreover, 'Jesus is not advising us to leave society and go into the desert. His counsel is that we should stay in society and set up in it communities which obey other rules and other laws. This advice rests on the conviction that we cannot change the phenomenon of power' (ibid., 62). So we should work within existing social structures and institutions, but at the same time change ourselves, our practices and behaviours, and build parallel communities free from the inequalities, violence and domination that characterise broader society. We should neither play the game of political power nor try to attack it directly, but rather work around and outside it. This emphasis on transforming oneself and one's relations with others, rather than attacking external social and political institutions directly, can be found, too, in the 'spiritual' anarchism of Gustav Landauer, who was in part inspired by the Christian mystic Meister Eckhardt. For Landauer, the state itself was a series of relationships, or a certain mode of relating to others, which was based on domination and the desire for power; therefore the state could be overcome by 'creating new social relationships; i.e., by people relating to one another differently' (Landauer, 2010: 213–14).

Profane Practices

There are many important and surprising parallels between anarchism and Christianity – among them also a certain cosmopolitan ethos, something that is particularly urgent today as borders go up, societies become increasingly insular and inhospitable, and populist politics mobilises itself around paranoid fantasies of national identity. At least in Christianity, the kingdom of God is potentially open to all. The cosmopolitan attitude – first expressed by the original anarchist, Diogenes of Sinope, who declared to Athenians that he was a 'citizen of the world' – is completely at odds with political theology, which is essentially concerned with defining and sacralising borders – conceptual, political, and ultimately national.

However, my broader point here was to develop the idea of a profane politics that would avoid the trap of political theology by refusing to be lured into the game of power. As I have suggested, this profane politics – which can draw on the resources of anarchism, Christianity, and indeed other religious and spiritual traditions – is based on an anarchic indifference to power and on the idea of transforming oneself and one's relations with others through the fostering of alternative practices, communities and ways of life. It is therefore very closely associated with Foucault's idea of 'counterconducts' and his interest in spiritual ascesis. One finds this, for instance, in some of the heretical movements of the Middle Ages, which, as in the case of Anabaptists or of the Brethren of the Free Spirit, had a distinctly antinomian, even anarchist tendency. Moreover, it seems to me that there is much to learn today from ascetic practices and from the forms of self-discipline and self-restraint that were important to Christianity, particularly in resisting the consumerist way of life, which not only harms the environment and wastes natural resources but also traps the subject within certain patterns of behaviour determined by the market and technology. There can be no hope of freedom without self-discipline, without the capacity to master one's appetites – an idea that was familiar to pagan Stoicism, ascetic Christianity, and, of course, many other religious traditions like Buddhism. Furthermore, the ideal and doctrine of apostolic poverty and humility, condemned as heretical by the church in the Middle Ages, could potentially serve as a model for a new attitude to life, one that resists unnecessary consumption in order to foster greater personal freedom and autonomy.

In developing this idea, the work of former priest Ivan Illich and his critique of industrial development and modern systems of healthcare and education are important. Writing in the 1970s, Illich argued that modern institutions had reached a point of crisis in efficiency and effectiveness. The root of the problem lay in our enslavement to machines and machine culture, as well as in our dependence on big institutions that robbed us of our autonomy. Central to Illich's critique of modern industrial society and its mania for economic and technological growth is the idea of negative returns (see Illich, 1975). When technology develops beyond a certain capacity, it starts to become inefficient and wasteful, and requires more time and energy to manage and use it; we have seen this today in the way in which the faster connectivity of communication networks and devices, which is supposed to save time, means only that we waste greater amounts of time 'staying connected'. The same rule of diminishing returns applies to modern medicine, which has not only taken responsibility for health away from people and placed it within big institutions and the pharmaceutical industry, but actually made people less healthy and more vulnerable to sickness, with more iatrogenic diseases and a greater reliance on drugs; for instance, we hear today about new, drug-resistant forms of bacteria, which have spawned owing to our overuse of antibiotics. The rule also applies, as Illich argues, to modern transport, which, once it exceeds a certain velocity, means that we spend more time travelling; the faster we can go, the slower we become, something that is obvious to any cyclist in a modern city whose speed far exceeds that of the cars stuck on congested roads.

There are a number of ideas here that are very important for our discussion of profane practice. Illich talks about new 'tools of conviviality' that would empower people and give them greater autonomy over their own lives – allowing them to reclaim control over work, technology, healthcare and learning. Resisting the institutionalisation of practices and forms of knowledge and reclaiming them for everyday – we could say profane – use would be an example of what Foucault has referred to as 'counterconducts'. As Illich puts it,

I choose the term 'conviviality' to designate the opposite of industrial productivity. I intend it to mean autonomous and creative intercourse among persons, and the intercourse of persons with their environment... I consider conviviality to be individual freedom realized in personal interdependence and, as such, an intrinsic ethical value. (Illich, 1975: 24)

Important here also is the emphasis on human limitation: not only will industrial and technological development and economic growth run up against their own internal limit, but also, in order to live sustainably and for society to achieve homeostasis, people will need to limit their own activity and consumption. They will need to reproduce less, consume less, work less, rely less on technology. However, rather than this being a miserable condition, it is something to be welcomed. Illich talks about a 'right to frugality' (ibid., 116). Taking Aquinas's dictum that austerity as a virtue does not exclude all pleasures, only those that are excessive and inordinate, beyond which there is scope for 'affability' (see Quaestio 168.3 in Aquinas, n.d.), Illich proposes that reducing our needless consumption and learning to live with simpler but more useful technology – coupled with a more just distribution of resources and power – would free up our time for self-expression and for more convivial relations with others: 'People will rediscover the value of joyful sobriety and liberating austerity only if they relearn to depend on each other rather than on energy slaves' (Illich, 1975: 27).

The problem is energy and its expenditure: the more energy and power produced and made available by machines and technology, the more energy and power are used, and the more we need. Therefore, for the sake of the survival of human as well as natural ecology, we need to limit our expenditure of energy and our addiction to technology. We need to break with the whole religion of limitless productivity, economic growth and technological progress.[4] This antidevelopment ethos, which recognises and indeed celebrates human limitation and lack – and advocates a simpler, more frugal and, for that reason, more joyful and convivial life – is another way of understanding what I call the profane. The profane is anti-Promethean in the sense that it calls into question the hubris of our belief in limitless human progress and scientific development and reminds us instead of our fragility, lack, and dependence upon the natural world we are in the process of destroying.

Today we see many such experiments in autonomy and conviviality, forms of practical utopianism where people, in international networks or local and regional communities, try to foster more worldly and profane ways of working, farming, consuming and living – whether it is the Slow Food or Slow Cities movements or movements around the world in defence of common natural resources, indigenous lands and the local environment against corporate and state enclosure and development. What these experiments all share is a desire to protect a profane 'living world' – in the form of local traditions and ways of life, and the natural environment – against the abstractions of an economic and industrial logic that sacrifices this world on the altar of profit and growth.

Apocalypse, *katechon*, and the Messianic Profane

The vision that haunts any analysis of political theology is the apocalypse – the scenario of the end of the world that is part of Christian eschatology and that, in our time, can only be understood in terms of catastrophic ecological collapse. The blind operation of the political–economic–technological machine, which sacrifices the living to the obscure gods of progress, growth and, ultimately, power, heads towards a moment of auto-destruction, as it comes up against its own disavowed natural limits. We are all complicit with this machine, yet have seemingly little control over its operation. The sense of an imminent end – or at least the long and maybe irreversible process of ecological and social deterioration and decline – is perhaps the reason for the mood of nihilism that pervades much of political and social life at the moment. There is a sense in which, behind the religious

frenzy and populist anger, behind the election of demagogues with their strange distortions of speech and truth,
behind the new puritanism and the hysterical moralisation
of public discourse, behind the crumbling façades of political
and financial institutions, there is an emptiness of meaning
and a growing despair, a terror at the void coupled with
a paralysis of effective action. Instead, a strange madness
or delirium, which perhaps was always lying beneath the
surface, has gripped societies – seen in increasingly deadly
mass shootings, terrorist attacks, technological addiction
and its associated mental illnesses, delusions of sovereignty
and fantasies of national identity, democratic endorsement
of infantile politics, and the spreading of hatred and division everywhere – all while global temperatures rise and
ecosystems collapse. This is the *danse macabre* at the end
of times.

The apocalypse in Christian eschatology – derived from
the Greek *apokalupsis*, meaning 'uncovering' – is associated
with the revelation of divine mysteries. In the prophecies
revealed to John on Patmos, the destruction of the world
would be followed by the salvation of the faithful in Christ's
kingdom. The description of the divine punishments visited
upon the world bears in our minds an eerie association with
ecological disasters; the revelations describe earthquakes,
plagues of fire, grasses and trees being burning up, waters
being poisoned, and so on.

According to the Apostle Paul in the Second Letter to the
Thessalonians, this series of events, leading to Christ's second
coming, would be preceded by the coming of the antichrist
or 'the lawless one', the one who falsely claims to be God
but who sets himself up against every religion. However, the
arrival of the antichrist would itself be held up by what Paul
called the 'restraining power' (or *katechon* – 'that which
withholds'): 'Evil is already insidiously at work but its activities are restricted until what I have called the "restraining
power" (of God) is removed' (2 Thessalonians 2.6–7; see also
the variant translation in Paul 2001–18). So the *katechon*
has a very ambiguous role in Christian eschatology: it

forestalls the arrival of the antichrist but, in doing so, it also delays the end of the world and Christ's second coming.

The *katechon* is a fundamental political category in Schmitt's thought. The role of 'restrainer' was played by the idea of the Christian empire in Europe in the Middle Ages, as the structure that preserved a certain geopolitical order, until this space was opened up by the discovery of the New World and the emergence of a new global political space (see Schmitt, 2006: 59–61). Moreover, we saw that the Catholic Church, with its representative image of the body of Christ, also had this symbolic function in the theological age. In the modern secular age, however, it is the sovereign state crystallised in the moment of the exception that, for Schmitt, restrains the apocalyptic threat posed by revolutionary anarchism. As Taubes claimed, the figure of the *katechon* is central to Schmitt's counterrevolutionary thought and his attempt to 'domesticate' the end of the world (Taubes, 2013: 13).

Can we say, however, that today these roles are now reversed? That it is sovereignty, and the politico-economic machine of which it is the escutcheon, that now hasten the end of the world; and that it is renewed forms of radical and anarchistic politics that, in seeking to preserve and care for the profane living world that currently exists, now act – as Benjamin put it – as the 'emergency brake' that puts a stop to the locomotive of 'progress'?[5] Benjamin's critique of the idea of progress and of the exploitation of humans and nature that progress involves is couched in terms of a Marxist materialist analysis of history. Yet it is not at all obvious that the Marxist tradition was not part of the very paradigm of industrial growth and technological development that is at issue here. Furthermore, Benjamin invokes the idea of revolution – while I have argued that the revolution, at least in the form of a totalising and transformative event, may no longer be the most suitable category for thinking about radical and oppositional politics today.

However, where I believe that Benjamin's thinking can be of help here is in his notion of the profane, which he relates to a messianic eschatology. He argues that the 'order of the profane should be erected on the idea of happiness' – a possibility I have tried to develop through the idea of conviviality. Yet how is the idea of profane happiness – something intrinsically worldly – reconcilable with messianism? As Benjamin says in his 'Theologico-Political Fragment',

> If one arrow points to the goal to which the profane dynamic acts, and another marks the direction of Messianic intensity, then certainly the quest of free humanity for happiness runs counter to the Messianic direction; but just as a force can, through acting, increase another that is acting in the opposite direction, so the order of the profane assists, through being profane, the coming of the Messianic Kingdom. (Benjamin, 1986b: 312–13)

Benjamin's messianism, based on the profane idea of happiness, is clearly very different from Christian eschatology – indeed, it is closer to the messianic traditions of Judaism. According to Benjamin, the Torah is not about speculating on the future – something prohibited by the Bible as sorcery – but about remembering the past. 'This does not imply, however,' as Benjamin says, 'that for the Jews the future became homogeneous, empty time. For every second was the small gateway in time through which the Messiah might enter' (Benjamin, 2003a).

Perhaps we can interpret this as an encouragement to act now, in the present moment, to transform ourselves and our immediate surroundings. If the Messiah can come at any time, then we can see every moment as an opening in which we have the freedom to think and act differently.

Jerusalem or Athens?

Like the two arrows fired in opposite directions in Benjamin's account of the messianic profane, the two opposing poles of Jerusalem and Athens – or theology and philosophy – have been the twin orientations this study has had to navigate between. Politics is at times pulled in one direction, at times in another. However, as we have seen, to extricate politics from the theological horizon – in which its truth is determined by revelation and its practice is based on blind faith and obedience to authority – and to reorient it around philosophy, we can actually draw on the resources of theology itself. In other words, theology, if no longer bound to the sacralisation of power, can become a way of affirming the eternal vocation of political philosophy – that is, the free and rational enquiry about how one should live.

Notes

Notes to Introduction

1　For a survey of various responses to the post-secular political condition, see de Vries and Sullivan (2006). For an earlier exploration of religion in the public space, see Casanova (1994).

2　A similar claim is made by Gianni Vattimo, who sees secularization, which reaches its high point in postmodern nihilism, as constituting the actual truth of Christianity, although his interpretation of Christianity in terms of *kenōsis* (κένωσις, 'emptying') – simultaneously a renunciation of its divine nature and a metaphysical notion of truth – is somewhat different from the notion of Christianity as eschatological salvation (see Rorty and Vattimo, 2005: 43–52).

3　I am alluding to the way in which members of the judiciary in the United Kingdom, who overruled the government in a court decision after the Brexit referendum, were denounced by the tabloid press as 'enemies of the people'.

Notes to Chapter 1

1　See also Bakunin (1882).

2　See Schmitt's later essay from 1929, 'The Age of Neutralizations and Depoliticizations' (Schmitt, 1963).

3 Indeed, the 'Röhm putsch' or 'Night of the Long Knives', which took place in the same year (1934) and which Schmitt, soon to be appointed as 'crown jurist' of the Third Reich, praised as an act in 'protection of the law', could be seen as a perfect embodiment of the sovereign state of exception, which is the central theme of *Political Theology*.

4 The state of exception that exceeds the law is a specific reference to the notorious Article 48 of the Weimar Constitution, which gave the president, in times of crisis, the authority to issue 'emergency decrees'. This was used by the Nazis to assume absolute power in 1933 and remained in place throughout their reign, thus effectively authorising a permanent state of emergency.

5 In fact, as Leo Strauss explains, liberalism is not Schmitt's real enemy; rather it is simply a neutral party and an obstacle to the real conflict with anarchism, and is hence treated with disdain rather than genuine enmity (see Strauss, in Schmitt, 2007: 99–122).

6 As Peterson put it in a letter to Friedrich Dessauer, it was written with the intention to 'deal a blow to *Reichstheologie*' (see Mrówczynski-van Allen, 2017: 11).

7 This would be a contested claim (see Crockett, 2003).

8 I would also refer readers here to the liberation theology that emerged in the Latin American context (e.g. Gutierrez, 1988).

Note to Chapter 2

1 This is associated with some of the mystical strands of Christianity, such as the ones to be found, for instance, in Dionysius the Areopagite's *Mystical Theology*.

Notes to Chapter 3

1 This similarity has been recognised by others (e.g. Reinhard, 2005: 11–75).

2 Eric Santner (2001) has used the term 'psychotheology' to refer to this nexus of politics, theology and the unconscious.

3 For Lacan, the unconscious is '*structured like a language*' (Lacan, 1981: 20).

4 This has been admirably illustrated by Santner (2011).

Notes to Chapter 4

1 Hobbes's debates with Bishop Bramhall on the idea of free will and determinism led to accusations that Hobbes's doctrine of necessity veered towards atheism. However, Michael Gillespie (2008) argues that Hobbes's determinism was in part influenced by the Calvinist doctrine of predestination. See also Martinich (1992).

2 Roberto Esposito has presented this logic of dividing and reuniting things in a relationship of 'exclusionary assimilation' – the incorporation of the Two into the One – as the central drive of what he calls the 'machine' of political theology, a theory that draws on Heidegger's theory of 'machination' (see Esposito, 2015).

3 Hobbes (1985: 269–70) says that the subject may 'without injustice' refuse to fight in war, although he may be punished for doing so. The heading of this section alludes to an interpretation of the figure of leviathan in the Middle Ages in which the great fish was a symbol of the devil, who is caught by God, as the fisherman, with a hook bated with Christ on the cross (see Schmitt, 1996a: 7–8).

4 This indeed is the gist of Strauss's critical charge against Schmitt (see Schmitt, 2007).

5 Here Schmitt's thinking displays clear overtones of anti-Semitism.

6 This is leaving aside the controversy over whether Kantorowicz's work can be seen as a veiled critique of the authoritarian conclusions of Schmitt's political theology (see Herrero, 2015).

7 That is, at least, if their wealth is any measure of their power. According to the latest market valuations, the wealth of the world's top five tech companies amounts to $2.9 trillion in total market capitalisation (see Desjardins, 2017).

8 See Wendy Brown's (2010) study of the current fetish for building walls, which, as a form of sovereign theatre, both masks and reveals the diminishing sovereignty of nation states.

9 'Post-truth' was apparently *the* word of 2016, according to the OED.

10 This at least is Agamben's claim, and he provides strong evidence to support it (see Agamben, 2005a: 52).

11 This is an expression that Benjamin used in his eighth thesis on the philosophy of history, in order to invoke the struggle against fascism, which has made the state of emergency no longer the exception, but the rule (see Benjamin, 1968: 253–64, 257).

12 The German noun *Gewalt* means 'violence', 'authority' and 'force'.

13 See James Martel's (2012) discussion of Benjamin's divine violence as a rejection of what he calls the political fetishism that sustains state sovereignty.

Notes to Chapter 5

1 Foucault (2007: 340) says that these emergency powers outside the law are like a 'permanent *coup d'état*'.

2 Indeed, Foucault mentions Stirner as one of the thinkers of the nineteenth century who attempted to reconstitute an ethics and an aesthetics of the self (see Foucault, 2005: 251).

3 See the comparison drawn by Plato in Book 9 of the *Republic* between the city under a tyrant and a soul dominated by a tyrannical nature; neither is free. Just as a city under a tyrant is miserable and enslaved, so the tyrant himself is miserable and enslaved to his own lawless passions (Plato 1973, in Benjamin Jowett's translation).

4 Of course, Foucault would be equally suspicious of the technocratic and scientific 'regimes of truth' that are under attack here. The classical discourse of the parrhesiast is neither one of technical expertise nor one that courts popular approval. The point is, however, that in this new political climate of 'post-truth' populism the prestige and hegemony of 'expert opinion' has been assailed to such an extent that, ironically, it is the technocrat and the scientist who now seem to embody the lonely and denigrated position of the parrhesiast going against the weight of public opinion.

5 The sermons of the Christian mystic Meister Eckhart are particularly interesting in this respect, invoking a total oneness with God: 'The eye with which I see God is exactly the same eye with which God sees me. My eye and God's eye are one eye, one seeing, one knowledge and one love' (Eckhart, 1994: Sermon 16).

6 Foucault reported on the revolution as a correspondent for *Corriere della Sera* and for *Le Nouvel Observateur*.
7 This is something for which Foucault was heavily criticised at the time (see Afary and Anderson, 2005).
8 *Un autre monde* (Foucault, 2011: 287).

Notes to Chapter 6

1 At times 'prosperity gospel' borders on a barely disguised scam. Creflo Dollar of Creflo Dollar Ministries put out a crowd-funding call to his followers to raise $65 million for a new Gulf Stream private jet so he could 'safely and swiftly share the Good News of the Gospel worldwide' (Blair, 2015).
2 For instance a study of graduate students at the University of Illinois found a link between mobile phone addiction and anxiety and depression (see Panova and Lleras, 2016).

Notes to Chapter 7

1 The distinction between secularisation and profanation is also made by Agamben, who says: 'Both are political operations: the first (secularisation) guarantees the exercise of power by carrying it back to the sacred model; the second (profanation) deactivates the apparatuses of power and returns to common use the spaces that power had seized' (Agamben, 2007: 77).
2 A similar idea can be found in 'process theology', which builds on the philosophy of Alfred North Whitehead and stresses interrelated processes rather than stable, immutable substances. Instead of God as an independent controlling power standing above creation, process theologians talk about the mutual dependency of living things and natural processes (see Cobb and Griffin, 1976).
3 See Reiner Schürmann's definition of anarchy, which he takes from Heidegger's idea of the closure of metaphysics: 'The anarchy that will be at issue here is the name of a history affecting the ground or foundation of action, a history where the bedrock yields and where it becomes obvious that the principle of cohesion, be it authoritarian or "rational", is no longer anything more than a blank space deprived of legislative, normative, power' (Schürmann, 1987: 6).

4 This idea is also reflected in what has come to be known as 'degrowth' (*décroissance*), an economic theory based on the idea of entropy that rejects the dogma of economic growth and calls for a new paradigm, based on ecological balance and limits to production and consumption (see Latouche, 2009; see also Georgescu-Roegen, 1975).

5 Benjamin (2003b: 402) actually says here 'locomotive of world history'.

References

Aquinas, T. (n.d.). 'Quaestio 168'. In idem, *Summa theologiae* II.2. Accessed 4 March 2018 at http://www.newadvent.org/summa/3168.htm#article4.

Afary, J. and Anderson, K. B. (2005). *Foucault and the Iranian Revolution: Gender and the Seductions of Islamism*. Chicago, IL: University of Chicago Press.

Agamben, G. (2005a). *State of Exception*, trans. by K. Attell. Chicago, IL: University of Chicago Press.

Agamben, G. (2005b). *The Time That Remains*, trans. by P. Dailey. Stanford, CA: Stanford University Press.

Agamben, G. (2007). *Profanations*. New York: Zone Books.

Agamben, G. (2011). *The Kingdom and the Glory: For a Theological Genealogy of Economy and Government (*Homo Sacer II, 2*)*, trans. by L. Chiesa. Stanford, CA: Stanford University Press.

Asad, T. (2003). *Formations of the Secular: Christianity, Islam, Modernity*. Stanford, CA: Stanford University Press.

Augustine of Hippo (2014). *The City of God*, vol. 1, ed. and trans. by Rev. Marcus Dodds. Project Gutenberg. Accessed 4 March 2018 at http://www.acatholic.org/wp-content/uploads/2014/06/The-City-of-God-Saint-Augustine.pdf.

Bakunin, M. (1871). *The Political Theology of Mazzini and the International*, trans. by S. E. Holmes. Accessed 4 March 2018 at http://wiki.libertarian-labyrinth.org/index.php?title=The_Political_Theology_of_Mazzini_and_the_International.

Bakunin, M. (1882). *God and the State*, trans. by B. R. Tucker. Accessed 4 March 2018 at https://theanarchistlibrary.org/library/michail-bakunin-god-and-the-state.

Becker, G. S. (1993). *Human Capital: A Theoretical and Empirical Analysis with Special Reference to Education*, 3rd edn. Chicago, IL: University of Chicago Press.

Benjamin, W. (1968). 'Theses on the Philosophy of History'. In idem, *Illuminations*, ed. by H. Arendt, trans. by H. Zohn. New York: Schocken Books, 253–64.

Benjamin, W. (1986a). 'Critique of Violence'. In idem, *Reflections: Essays, Aphorisms, Autobiographical Writings*, ed. by P. Demetz, trans. by E. Jephcott. New York: Schocken Books, 277–300.

Benjamin, W. (1986b). 'Theologico-Political Fragment'. In idem, *Reflections: Essays, Aphorisms, Autobiographical Writings*, ed. by P. Demetz, trans. by E. Jephcott. New York: Schocken Books, 312–13.

Benjamin, W. (1996). 'Capitalism as Religion'. In idem, *Selected Writings, 1913–1926*, ed. by M. Bullock and M. W. Jennings. Cambridge, MA: Harvard University Press, 228–91.

Benjamin, W. (1998). *The Origin of German Tragic Drama*, trans. by J. Osborne. London: Verso.

Benjamin, W. (2003a) 'On the Concept of History'. In idem, *Selected Writings*, vol. 4: 1938–1940, ed. by H. Eiland and M. W. Jennings, trans. by E. Jephcott. Cambridge, MA: Harvard University Press, 389–400.

Benjamin, W. (2003b). 'Paralipomena to "On the Concept of History"'. In *Selected Writings*, vol. 4: 1938–1940, ed. by H. Eiland and M. W. Jennings, trans. by E. Jephcott. Cambridge, MA: Harvard University Press, 401–11.

Berardi, F. (2009). *The Soul at Work: From Alienation to Autonomy*, trans. by F. Cadel and G. Mecchia. Cambridge, MA: MIT Press.

Blair, L. (2015). 'Televangelist Creflo Dollar Needs 200,000 People to Donate $300 Each So He Can Buy $65M Ministry Plane: Churches Will Have to Foot Part of Fuel Bill'. *The Christian Post*, 12 March. Accessed 7 April 2018 at https://www.christianpost.com/news/televangelist-creflo-dollar-needs-200000-people-to-donate-300-each-so-he-can-buy-65m-ministry-plane-135582.

Blumenberg, H. (1985). *The Legitimacy of the Modern Age*, trans. by R. M. Wallace. Cambridge, MA: MIT Press.

Bookchin, M. (1982). *The Ecology of Freedom: The Emergence and Dissolution of Hierarchy*. Paolo Alto, CA: Cheshire Books.

Borradori, G. (2003). *Philosophy in a Time of Terror: Dialogues with Jurgen Habermas and Jacques Derrida*. Chicago, IL: University of Chicago Press.

Brown, W. (2010). *Walled States, Waning Sovereignty*. New York: Zone Books.

Casanova, J. (1994). *Public Religions in the Modern World*. Chicago, IL: Chicago University Press.

Catechism of the Catholic Church (n.d). 'Sacred Scripture' [Article 3 in Part One, Section One, Chapter Two]. Accessed 5 March 2018 at http://www.vatican.va/archive/ccc_css/archive/catechism/p1s1c2a3.htm.

Cobb, J. B., Jr and Griffin, D. R. (1976). *Process Theology: An Introductory Exposition*. Philadelphia, PA: Westminster Press.

Connolly, W. E. (2005). 'The Evangelical–Capitalist Resonance Machine'. *Political Theory* 33 (6): 869–86.

Crockett, C. (2003). *Radical Political Theology*. Columbia, SC: Columbia University Press.

de La Boétie, É. (1942) [1548]. *Discourse on Voluntary Servitude*, trans. by H. Kurz. New York: Columbia University Press.

de La Mettrie, J. O. (1996). *Machine Man and Other Writings*, ed. by A. Thomson. Cambridge: Cambridge University Press.

de Tocqueville, A. (2010). *Democracy in America*, ed. by E. Nolla, trans. by J. T. Schleifer. Indianapolis, IN: Liberty Fund.

de Vries, H. and Sullivan, L. E., eds (2006). *Political Theologies: Public Religions in a Post-Secular World*. New York: Fordham University Press.

Deleuze, G. (1992). 'Postscript on the Societies of Control'. *October* 59: 3–7.

Derrida, J. (1998). 'Faith and Knowledge: Two Sources of "Religion" at the Limits of Reason Alone'. In J. Derrida and G. Vattimo, *Religion*. Cambridge: Polity, 1–78.

Derrida, J. (2005). *Rogues: Two Essays on Reason*, trans. by P.-A. Brault and M. Naas. Stanford, CA: Stanford University Press.

Desjardins, J. (2017). 'Here's How the Top 5 Tech Giants Make Their Billions'. *Business Insider UK*, 16 May. Accessed 5 March 2018 at http://uk.businessinsider.com/heres-how-the-top-5-tech-giants-make-their-billions-2017–5?r=US&IR=T.

Dionysius the Areopagite (n.d.). *Mystical Theology*. Accessed 5 March 2018 at http://www.esoteric.msu.edu/VolumeII/MysticalTheology.html.

Eckhart, M. (1994). *Selected Writings*, trans. by O. Davies. London: Penguin.

Ellul, J. (1964). *The Technological Society*, trans. by J. Wilkinson. New York: Vintage Books.

Ellul, J. (1975). *The New Demons*, trans. by C. E. Hopkin. New York: Seabury Press.

Ellul, J. (1991). *Anarchy and Christianity*, trans. by G. Bromiley. Grand Rapids, MI: Eerdmans Publishing.

Esposito, R. (2011). *Immunitas: The Protection and Negation of Life*. Cambridge: Polity.

Esposito, R. (2015). *Two: The Machine of Political Theology and the Place of Thought*, trans. by Z. Hanafi. New York: Fordham University Press.

Feuerbach, L. (1957). *The Essence of Christianity*, trans. by G. Eliot. New York: Harper & Row.

Foucault, M. (1978). *The History of Sexuality*, vol. 1: Introduction, trans. by R. Hurley. New York: Pantheon Books.

Foucault, M. (1991). *Discipline and Punish: The Birth of the Prison*, trans. by A. Sheridan. London: Penguin.

Foucault, M. (2002a). 'Truth and Power'. In idem, *Power*, vol. 3 of *Essential Works of Foucault, 1954–1984*, ed. by J. Faubion, trans. by R. Hurley. London: Penguin, 111–33.

Foucault, M. (2002b). 'Useless to Revolt?' In idem, *Power*, vol. 3 of *Essential Works of Foucault, 1954–1984*, ed. by J. Faubion, trans. by R. Hurley. London: Penguin, 449–53.

Foucault, M. (2002c). 'The Subject and Power'. In idem, *Power*, vol. 3 of *Essential Works of Foucault, 1954–1984*, ed. by J. Faubion, trans. by R. Hurley. London: Penguin, 326–48.

Foucault, M. (2003). *Society Must Be Defended: Lectures at the Collège de France, 1975–1976*, ed. by M. Bertani and A. Fontana, trans. by D. Macey. London: Allen Lane.

Foucault, M. (2005). *The Hermeneutics of the Subject: Lectures at the Collège de France, 1981–1982*, ed. by F. Gros, trans. by G. Burchell. Basingstoke: Palgrave Macmillan.

Foucault, M. (2007). *Security, Territory, Population: Lectures at the Collège de France, 1977–1978*, ed. by M. Senellart, trans. by G. Burchell. Basingstoke: Palgrave Macmillan.

Foucault, M. (2010a). *The Birth of Biopolitics: Lectures at the Collge de France, 1978–1979*, ed. by M. Senellart, trans. by G. Burchell. New York: Palgrave Macmillan.

Foucault, M. (2010b). *The Government of the Self and Others: Lectures at the Collège de France, 1982–1983*, ed. by F. Gros, trans. by G. Burchell. Basingstoke: Palgrave Macmillan.

Foucault, M. (2011). *The Courage of Truth: Lectures at the Collège de France, 1983–1984*, ed. by F. Gros, trans. by G. Burchell. Basingstoke: Palgrave Macmillan.

Foucault, M. (2014). *Wrong-Doing, Truth-Telling: The Function of Avowal in Justice*, ed. by F. Brion and B. Harcourt, trans. by S. Sawyer. Chicago, IL: University of Chicago Press.

Freud, S. (1939). *Moses and Monotheism*, trans. by K. Jones. London: Hogarth Press/Institute of Psychoanalysis.

Freud, S. (1949). *Group Psychology and the Analysis of the Ego*, trans. by J. Strachey. London: Hogarth Press.

Freud, F. (1961a). *Civilization and Its Discontents*, trans. by J. Strachey. New York: Norton.

Freud, S. (1961b). *The Future of an Illusion*, ed. and trans. by J. Strachey. New York: Norton.

Freud, S. (2001). *Totem and Taboo: Some Points of Agreement between the Mental Lives of Savages and Neurotics*, trans. by J. Strachey. London: Routledge.

Georgescu-Roegen, N. (1975). 'Energy and Economic Myths'. *Southern Economic Journal* 41 (3): 347–81.

Gillespie, M. A. (2008). *The Theological Origins of Modernity*. Chicago, IL: University of Chicago Press.

Gutierrez, G. (1988). *A Theology of Liberation: History, Politics and Salvation*, 15th edn. Maryknowll, NY: Orbis Books.

Habermas, J. (2003). *The Future of Human Nature*. Cambridge: Polity.

Habermas, J. (2008). 'Notes on Post-Secular Society'. *New Perspectives Quarterly* 25 (4): 17–29.

Hegel, G. W. F. (2001a). *The Philosophy of History*, trans. by J. Sibree. Kitchener, Ireland: Batoche Books.

Hegel, G. W. F. (2001b). *Philosophy of Right*, trans. by S. W Dyde. Kitchener, Ireland: Batoche Books.

Hegel, G. W. F. (2011). *Lectures on the Philosophy of World History*, vol. 1, ed. and trans. by R. F. Brown and P. C. Hodgson. Oxford: Clarendon.

Herrero, M. (2015). 'On Political Theology: The Hidden Dialogue between C. Schmitt and Ernst H. Kantorowicz in *The King's Two Bodies*'. *History of European Ideas* 41 (8): 1164–77.

Hobbes, T. (1985). *Leviathan*, ed. by C. B. Macpherson. London: Penguin.

Hollenbach, D. (2004). *The Common Good and Christian Ethics*. Cambridge: Cambridge University Press.

Illich, I. (1975). *Tools for Conviviality*. New York: Fontana/ Collins.

Kantorowicz, E. H. (1997). *The King's Two Bodies: A Study in Medieval Political Theology*. Princeton, NJ: Princeton University Press.

Kelsen, H. (1967). *Pure Theory of Law*, trans. by M. Knight. Berkeley, CA: University of California Press.

Lacan, J. (1981). *The Seminar of Jacques Lacan, Book XI: The Four Fundamental Concepts of Psychoanalysis*, ed. by J.-A. Miller, trans. by A. Sheridan. New York: Norton.

Lacan, J. (1993). *The Seminar of Jacques Lacan, Book III: The Psychoses, 1955–1956*, ed. by J.-A. Miller, trans. by R. Grigg. New York: Norton.

Lacan, J. (1997). *The Seminar of Jacques Lacan, Book VII: The Ethics of Psychoanalysis, 1959–1960*, ed. by J.-A. Miller, trans. by D. Potter. New York: Norton.

Lacan, J. (1999). *The Seminar of Jacques Lacan, Book XX (Encore 1972–1973): On Feminine Sexuality; The Limits of Love and Knowledge*, trans. by B. Fink. New York: Norton.

Lacan, J. (2006). 'Kant with Sade', in idem, *Écrits*, trans. by B. Fink. New York: Norton, 645–67.

Lacan, J. (2007). *The Seminar of Jacques Lacan, Book XVII: The Other Side of Psychoanalysis*, ed. by J.-A. Miller, trans. by R. Grigg. New York: Norton.

Lacan, J. (2013). *The Triumph of Religion; Preceded by Discourse to Catholics*, trans. by B. Fink. Cambridge: Polity.

Landauer, G. (2010). 'Weak State, Weaker People'. In *Revolution and Other Writings: A Political Reader*, ed. and trans. by G. Kuhn. Oakland, CA: PM Press.

Latouche, S. (2009). *Farewell to Growth*, trans. by D. Macey. Cambridge: Polity.

Lazzarato, M. (2012). *The Making of the Indebted Man: An Essay on the Neoliberal Condition*, trans. by J. D. Jordan. New York: Semiotext(e).

Lefort, C. (2006). 'The Permanence of the Theologico-Political?' In *Political Theologies: Public Religions in a Post-Secular World*, ed. by H. De Vries and L. E. Sullivan. New York: Fordham University Press, 148–87.

Löwith, K. (1949). *Meaning in History*. Chicago, IL: University of Chicago Press.

Martel, J. (2012). *Divine Violence: Walter Benjamin and the Eschatology of Sovereignty*. Abingdon: Routledge.

Martinich, A. P. (1992). *The Two Gods of Leviathan: Thomas Hobbes and Religion and Politics*. Cambridge: Cambridge University Press.

Marx, K. (1930). *Capital: A Critique of Political Economy*, vol. 1, trans. by E. Paul and C. Paul. London: Dent.

Marx, K. (1978). 'On the Jewish Question'. In *The Marx–Engels Reader*, ed. by R. Tucker. New York: Norton, 26–46.

Meier, H. (1995). *Carl Schmitt and Leo Strauss: The Hidden Dialogue*, trans. by J. Harvey Lomax. Chicago, IL: University of Chicago Press.

Meier, H. (1998). *The Lesson of Carl Schmitt: Four Chapters on the Distinction between Political Theology and Political Philosophy*, trans. by M. Brainard. Chicago, IL: University of Chicago Press.

Meier, H. (2006). *Leo Strauss and the Theologico-Political Problem*, trans. by M. Brainard. Cambridge: Cambridge University Press.

Metz, J. B. (1998). *Passion for God: The Mystical Political Dimension of Christianity*, trans. by J. M. Ashley. Mahwah, NJ: Paulist Press.

Mevorach, S. (2015). *Kabbalah and Ecology: God's Image in a More-Than-Human World*. Cambridge: Cambridge University Press.

Moltmann, J. (1985). *God in Creation: An Ecological Doctrine of Creation: The Gifford Lectures, 1984–1985*. London: SCM Press.

Moltmann, J. (1999). *God for a Secular Society: The Public Relevance of Theology*, trans. by M. Kohl. London: SCM Press.

Moore, M. (2008). 'Religious Leaders Blame Bankers' Greed for Financial Crisis'. *Telegraph*, 25 December. Accessed 6 March 2018 at http://www.telegraph.co.uk/news/religion/3949359/Religious-leaders-blame-bankers-greed-for-financial-crisis.html.

Mouffe, C. (2009). *The Democratic Paradox*. London: Verso.
Moyo, D. (2017). 'Global Debt Woes Are Building Up to a Tidal Wave'. *Financial Times*, 29 May. Accessed 6 March 2018 at https://www.ft.com/content/3215e960–3faa-11e7–9d56–25f963e998b2.
Mrówczynski-van Allen, A. (2017). 'Beyond Political Theology and Its Liquidation: From Theopolitical Monotheism to Trinitarianism'. *Modern Theology*. DOI: 10.1111/moth12356.
Mumford, L. (1934). *Technics and Civilization*. London: Routledge & Kegan Paul.
Nelson, R. E. (2001). *Economics as Religion: From Samuelson to Chicago and Beyond*. University Park, PA: University of Pennsylvania Press.
Nietzsche, F. (1989). *On the Genealogy of Morals*, trans. by W. Kaufmann and R. J. Hollingdale. New York: Vintage Books.
Osteen, J. (2004). *Your Best Life Now: 7 Steps to Living at Your Full Potential*. New York: Faith Words.
Panova, T. and Lleras, A. (2016). 'Avoidance or Boredom: Negative Mental Health Outcomes Associated with Use of Information and Communication Technologies Depend on Users' Motivations'. *Computers in Human Behaviour* 58: 249–58.
Paul (2001–18). '2 Thessalonians: Paul's Second Letter to the Thessalonians'. Early Christian Writings. Accessed 6 March 2018 at http://www.earlychristianwritings.com/text/2thessalonians-web.html.
Peterson, E. (2011). *Theological Tractates*, ed. and trans. by M. J. Hollerich. Stanford, CA: Stanford University Press.
Plato. (1973). *The Republic*, trans. by B. Jowett. New York: Anchor.
Pocock, J. G. A. (1989). *Politics, Language, and Time: Essays on Political Thought and History*. Chicago, IL: University of Chicago Press.
Rawls, J. (2005). *Political Liberalism*. New York: Columbia University Press.
Reinhard, K. (2005). 'Toward a Political Theology of the Neighbor'. In S. Žižek, E. L. Santner and K. Reinhard, *The Neighbor: Three Enquiries in Political Theology*. Chicago, IL: University of Chicago Press, 11–75.
Rodionova, Z. (2016). 'How Tesla Boss Elon Musk Works up to 100 Hours a Week'. *Independent*, 27 January. Accessed 6 March 2018 at http://www.independent.co.uk/news/business/

news/how-boss-elon-musk-works-up-to-100-hours-a-week-a6836461.html.

Rorty, R. and Vattimo, G. (2005). *The Future of Religion*, ed. by S. Zabala. New York: Columbia University Press.

Santner, E. L. (2001). *On the Psychotheology of Everyday Life*. Chicago, IL: University of Chicago Press.

Santner, E. L. (2011). *The Royal Remains: The People's Two Bodies and the Endgames of Sovereignty*. Chicago, IL: University of Chicago Press.

Schmitt, C. (1963). 'The Age of Neutralizations and Depoliticizations', trans. by M. Konzett and J. F. McCormic. In idem, *Der Begrzff des Politischen: Text von 1932 mit einem Vorruort und drei Corollarien*. Berlin: Dunker & Hurnblot, 79–95.

Schmitt, C. (1996a). *The Leviathan in the State Theory of Thomas Hobbes: The Meaning and Failure of a Political Symbol*, trans. by G. Schwab and E. Hilfstein. Westport, CT: Greenwood Press.

Schmitt, C. (1996b). *Roman Catholicism and Political Form*, trans. by G. L. Ulmen. Westport, CT: Greenwood Press.

Schmitt, C. (2000). *The Crisis of Parliamentary Democracy*, trans. by E. Kennedy. Cambridge, MA: MIT Press.

Schmitt, C. (2005). *Political Theology: Four Chapters on the Concept of Sovereignty*, trans. by G. Schwab. Chicago, IL: University of Chicago Press, 2005.

Schmitt, C. (2006). *The* Nomos *of the Earth in the International Law of the* Jus Publicum Europeaum, trans. by G. L. Ulmen. New York: Telos Press.

Schmitt, C. (2007). *The Concept of the Political*, trans. by G. Schwab. Chicago, IL: University of Chicago Press.

Schmitt, C. (2008). *Constitutional Theory*, trans. by J. Seitzer. Durham, NC: Duke University Press.

Schmitt, C. (2017). *Ex captivitate salus*, trans. by M. Hannah. Cambridge: Polity.

Schürmann, R. (1987). *Heidegger on Being and Acting: From Principles to Anarchy*, trans. by C.-M. Gros. Bloomington: Indiana University Press.

Smith, A. (1984). *The Theory of Moral Sentiments*, ed. by D. D. Raphael and A. L. Macfie. Indianapolis, IN: Liberty Fund.

Sorel, G. (2004). *Reflections on Violence*, ed. by J. Jennings. Cambridge: Cambridge University Press.

Spinoza, B. (2007). *Theological–Political Treatise*, ed. by J. Israel. Cambridge: Cambridge University Press.

Stimilli, E. (2017). *The Debt of the Living: Ascesis and Capitalism*, trans. by A. Bove. Albany, NY: SUNY Press.

Stirner, M. (1995). *The Ego and Its Own*, ed. by D. Leopold, trans. by S. Byington. Cambridge: Cambridge University Press.

Strauss, L. (1957). 'What Is Political Philosophy?'. *Journal of Political Philosophy* 19 (3): 343–68.

Strauss, L. (1967). 'Jerusalem and Athens: Some Introductory Reflections'. *Commentary* 43 (6): 45–57.

Strauss, L. (1982). *Spinoza's Critique of Religion*, trans. by E. M. Sinclair. New York: Schocken Books.

Strauss, L. (2007). 'What Can We Learn from Political Theory?'. *Review of Politics* 69 (4): 515–29.

Suarez-Villa, L. (2009). *Technocapitalism: A Critical Perspective on Technological Innovation and Corporatism*. Philadelphia, PA: Temple University Press.

Taubes, J. (2003). *The Political Theology of Paul*. Stanford, CA: Stanford University Press.

Taubes, J. (2010). *From Cult to Culture: Fragments Towards a Critique of Historical Reason*, ed. by C. E. Fonrobert and A. Engel. Stanford, CA: Stanford University Press.

Taubes, J. (2013). *To Carl Schmitt: Letters and Reflections*, trans. by K. Tribe. New York: Columbia University Press.

Taylor, C. (2007). *A Secular Age*. Cambridge, MA: Harvard University Press.

Thompson, N. (2017). 'Our Minds Have Been Hijacked by Our Phones: Tristan Harris Wants to Rescue Them'. Interview with Tristan Harris. *Wired*, 27 July. Accessed 24 March 2018 at https://www.wired.com/story/our-minds-have-been-hijacked-by-our-phones-tristan-harris-wants-to-rescue-them.

Tucker, R. C., ed. (1978). *The Marx–Engels Reader*, 2nd edn. New York: Norton.

Uglino, B. (n.d.). *The Little Flowers of St Francis of Assisi*. Christian Classics Ethereal Library. Accessed 24 March 2018 at https://www.ccel.org/ccel/ugolino/flowers.toc.html.

van Nuffelen, P. (2010). 'Varro's *Divine Antiquities*: Roman Religion as an Image of Truth'. *Classical Philology* 105 (2): 162–88.

Weber, M. (2001). *The Protestant Ethic and the Spirit of Capitalism*, trans. by T. Parsons. London: Routledge.

White, L. (1967). 'The Historical Roots of Our Ecological Crisis'. *Science* 155 (3767): 1203–7.

Index